IMMORTAL MEMORIES

CLEMENT SHORTER

1st WORLD
LIBRARY
Literary Society

Immortal Memories

Clement Shorter

© 1st World Library, 2007
PO Box 2211
Fairfield, IA 52556
www.1stworldlibrary.com
First Edition

LCCN: 2007934103

Softcover ISBN: 978-1-4218-9634-2
Hardcover ISBN: 978-1-4218-9734-9
eBook ISBN: 978-1-4218-9534-5

Purchase *"Immortal Memories"*
as a traditional bound book at:
www.1stWorldLibrary.com/purchase.asp?ISBN=978-1-4218-9634-2

1ˢᵗ World Library Literary Society

Giving Back to the World

"If you want to work on the core problem, it's early school literacy."

- **James Barksdale, former CEO of Netscape**

"No skill is more crucial to the future of a child, or to a democratic and prosperous society, than literacy."

- **Los Angeles Times**

"Literacy... means far more than learning how to read and write... The aim is to transmit... knowledge and promote social participation."

- **UNESCO**

"Literacy is not a luxury, it is a right and a responsibility. If our world is to meet the challenges of the twenty-first century we must harness the energy and creativity of all our citizens."

- **President Bill Clinton**

"Parents should be encouraged to read to their children, and teachers should be equipped with all available techniques for teaching literacy, so the varying needs and capacities of individual kids can be taken into account."

- **Hugh Mackay**

PREFATORY

The following addresses were delivered at the request of various literary societies and commemorative committees. They amused me to write, and they apparently interested the audiences for which they were primarily intended. Perhaps they do not bear an appearance in print. But they are not for my brother-journalists to read nor for the judicious men of letters. I prefer to think that they are intended solely for those whom Hazlitt styled "sensible people." Hazlitt said that "the most sensible people to be met with in society are men of business and of the world." I am hoping that these will buy my book and that some of them will like it.

It is recorded by Sir Henry Taylor of Samuel Rogers that when he wrote that very indifferent poem, *Italy*, he said, "I will make people buy. Turner shall illustrate my verse." It is of no importance that the biographer of Rogers tells us that the poet first made the artist known to the world by these illustrations. Taylor's story is a good one, and the moral worth taking to heart. The late Lord Acton, most learned and most accomplished of men, wrote out a list of the hundred best books as he considered them to be. They were printed in a popular magazine. They naturally excited much interest. I have rescued them from the pages of the *Pall Mall Magazine*. Those who will not buy my book for its seven other essays may do so on account of Lord Acton's list of books being here first preserved "between boards." I shall be equally well pleased.

CLEMENT SHORTER.

GREAT MISSENDEN, BUCKS.

I

TO THE IMMORTAL MEMORY OF
DR. SAMUEL JOHNSON

A toast proposed at the Johnson Birthday Celebration held at the Three Crowns Inn, Lichfield, in September, 1906.

In rising to propose this toast I cannot ignore what must be in many of your minds, the recollection that last year it was submitted by a very dear friend of my own, who, alas! has now gone to his rest, I mean Dr. Richard Garnett. {3} Many of you who heard him in this place will recall, with kindly memories, that venerable scholar. I am one of those who, in the interval have stood beside his open grave; and I know you will permit me to testify here to the fact that rarely has such brilliant scholarship been combined with so kindly a nature, and with so much generosity to other workers in the literary field. One may sigh that it is not possible to perpetuate for all time for the benefit of others the vast mass of learning which such men as Dr. Garnett are able to accumulate. One may lament even more that one is not able to present in some concrete form, as an example to those who follow, his fine qualities of heart and mind—his generous faculty for 'helping lame dogs over stiles.'

Dr. Garnett had not only a splendid erudition that specially qualified him for proposing this toast, he had also what many of you may think an equally exceptional qualification—he was a native of Lichfield; he was born in this fine city. As a Londoner—like Boswell when charged with the crime of being a Scotsman I may say that I cannot help it—I suppose I should come to you with hesitating footsteps. Perhaps it was rash of me to come at all, in spite of an invitation so kindly worded. Yet how gladly does any lover, not only of Dr. Johnson, but of all good literature, come to Lichfield. Four cathedral cities of our land stand forth in my mind with a certain magnetic power to draw even the most humble lover of books towards them—Oxford, Bath, Norwich, Lichfield, these four and no others. Oxford we all love and revere as the nourishing mother of so many famous men. Here we naturally recall Dr. Johnson's love of it—his defence of it against all comers. The glamour of Oxford and the memory of the great men who from age to age have walked its streets and quadrangles, is with us upon every visit. Bath again has noble memories. Upon house after house in that fine city is inscribed the fact that it was at one time the home of a famous man or woman of the past. Through its streets many of our great imaginative writers have strolled, and those streets have been immortalized in the pages of several great novelists, notably of Jane Austen and Charles Dickens.

For the City of Norwich I have a particular affection, as for long the home in quite separate epochs of Sir Thomas Browne and of George Borrow. I recall that in the reign of one of its Bishops—the father of Dean Stanley—there was a literary circle of striking character, that men and women of intellect met in the episcopal palace to discuss all 'obstinate questionings.'

But if he were asked to choose between the golden age of Bath, of Norwich, or of Lichfield, I am sure that any man

Clement Shorter

who knew his books would give the palm to Lichfield, and would recall that period in the life of Lichfield when Dr. Seward resided in the Bishop's Palace, with his two daughters, and when they were there entertaining so many famous friends. I saw the other day the statement that Anna Seward's name was unknown to the present generation. Now I have her works in nine volumes {6}; I have read them, and I doubt not but that there are many more who have done the same. Sir Walter Scott's friendship would alone preserve her memory if every line she wrote deserved to be forgotten as is too readily assumed. Scott, indeed, professed admiration for her verse, and a yet greater poet, Wordsworth, wrote in praise of two fine lines at the close of one of her sonnets, that entitled 'Invitation to a Friend,' lines which I believe present the first appearance in English poetry of the form of blank verse immortalized by Tennyson.

> Come, that I may not hear the winds of night,
> Nor count the heavy eave-drops as they fall.

"You have well criticized the poetic powers of this lady," says Wordsworth, "but, after all, her verses please me, with all their faults, better than those of Mrs. Barbauld, who, with much higher powers of mind, was spoiled as a poetess by being a dissenter."

Less, however, can be said for her poetry to-day than for her capacity as a letter writer. A letter writing faculty has immortalized more than one English author, Horace Walpole for example, who had this in common with Anna Seward, that he had the bad taste not to like Dr. Johnson.

Sooner or later there will be a reprint of a selection of Anna Seward's correspondence; you will find in it a picture of country life in the middle of the eighteenth century—and by that I mean Lichfield life—that is quite unsurpassed. Anna

Seward, her friends and her enemies, stand before us in very marked outline. As with Walpole also, she must have written with an eye to publication. Veracity was not her strong point, but her literary faculty was very marked indeed. Those who have read the letters that treat of her sister's betrothal and death, for example, will not easily forget them. The accepted lover, you remember, was a Mr. Porter, a son of the widow whom Johnson married; and Sarah Seward, aged only eighteen, died soon after her betrothal to him. That is but one of a thousand episodes in the world into which we are introduced in these pages. {8}

The Bishop's Palace was the scene of brilliant symposiums. There one might have met Erasmus Darwin of the *Botanic Garden*, whose fame has been somewhat dulled by the extraordinary genius of his grandson. There also came Richard Edgeworth, the father of Maria, whose *Castle Rackrent* and *The Absentee* are still among the most delightful books that we read; and there were the two young girls, Honora and Elizabeth Sneyd, who were destined in succession to become Richard Edgeworth's wives. There, above all, was Thomas Day, the author of *Sanford and Merton*, a book which delighted many of us when we were young, and which I imagine with all its priggishness will always survive as a classic for children. There, for a short time, came Major Andre, betrothed to Honora Sneyd, but destined to die so tragically in the American War of Independence. It is to Miss Seward's malicious talent as a letter writer that we owe the exceedingly picturesque account of Day's efforts to obtain a wife upon a particular pattern, his selection of Sabrina Sidney, whom he prepared for that high destiny by sending her to a boarding school until she was of the right age—his lessons in stoicism—his disappointment because she screamed when he fired pistols at her petticoats, and yelled when he dropped melted sealing-wax on her bare arms; it is a tragi-comic picture, and one is glad that Sabrina married some other man than her exacting guardian. But we would not miss Miss Seward's racy stories for anything, nor ignore her many letters with their revelation of the glories of old- time Lichfield, and of those 'lunar meetings' at which the wise ones foregathered. Now and again these worthies burst into sarcasm at one another's expense, as when Darwin satirizes the publication of Mr. Seward's edition of *Beaumont and Fletcher*, and Dr. Johnson's edition of *Shakspere*

> From Lichfield famed two giant critics come,
> Tremble, ye Poets! hear them! Fe, Fo, Fum!
> By Seward's arm the mangled Beaumont bled,
> And Johnson grinds poor Shakspere's bones for bread.

But perhaps after all, if we eliminate Dr. Johnson, the lover of letters gives the second place, not to Miss Seward and her circle, but to David Garrick. Lichfield contains more than one memento of that great man. The actor's art is a poor sort of thing as a rule. Johnson, in his tarter moments, expresses this attitude, as when he talked of Garrick as a man who exhibited himself for a shilling, when he called him 'a futile fellow,' and implied that it was very unworthy of Lord Campden to have made much of the actor and to have ignored so distinguished a writer as Goldsmith, when thrown into the company of both. Still undoubtedly Johnson's last word upon Garrick is the best—'his death has eclipsed the gaiety of nations and diminished the public stock of harmless pleasure.' We who live more than a hundred years later are able to recognize that Garrick has been the one great actor from that age to this. As a rule the mummers are mimics and little more, and generations go on, giving them their brief but glorious hour of fame, and then leaving them as mere names in the history of the stage. Garrick was preserved from this fate, not only by the circumstance that he had an army of distinguished literary friends, but by his interesting personality and by his own writings. Many lines of his plays and prologues have become part of current speech. Moreover his must have been a great personality, as those of us who have met Sir Henry Irving in these latter days have realized that his was also a great personality. It is fitting, therefore, that these two great actors, the most famous of an interesting, if not always an heroic profession, should lie side by side in Westminster Abbey.

I now come to my toast "The memory of Dr. Johnson." After all, Johnson was the greatest of all Lichfieldians, and one of the great men of his own and of all ages. We may talk about him and praise him because we shall be the better for so doing, but we shall certainly say nothing new. One or two points, however, seem to me worthy of emphasis in this company of Johnsonians. I think we should resent two popular fallacies which you will not hear from literary students, but only from one whom it is convenient to call "the man in the street." The first is, that we should know nothing about Johnson if it were not for Boswell's famous life, and the second that Johnson the author is dead, and that our great hero only lives as a brilliant conversationalist in the pages of Boswell and others. Boswell's *Life of Johnson* is the greatest biography in the English language; we all admit that. It is crowded with incident and anecdote. Neither Walter Scott nor Rousseau, each of whom has had an equal number of pages devoted to his personality, lives so distinctly for future ages as does Johnson in the pages of Boswell. Understanding all this, we are entitled to ask ourselves what we should have thought of Dr. Johnson had there been no Boswell; and to this question I do not hesitate to answer that we should have loved him as much as ever, and that there would still have been a mass of material with the true Boswellian flavour. He would not have made an appeal to so large a public, but some ingenious person would have drawn together all the anecdotes, all the epigrams, all the touches of that fine humanity, and given us from these various sources an amalgam of Johnson, that every bookman at least would have desired to read and study. In Fanny Burney's *Letters and Diaries* the presentation of Johnson is delightful. I wonder very much that all the Johnson fragments that Miss Burney provides have not been published separately. Then Mrs. Thrale has chatted about Johnson copiously in her "Anecdotes," and these pleasant stories have been reprinted again and again for the curious. I recall many other sources of information about the great man and his wonderful talk— by Miss Hawkins, Miss Reynolds, Miss Hannah More for example—and many of you who have Dr. Birkbeck Hill's *Johnson Miscellanies* have these in a pleasantly acceptable form.

My second point is concerned with Dr. Johnson's position apart from all this fund of anecdote, and this brilliant collection of unforgettable epigram in Boswell and elsewhere. As a writer, many will tell you, Dr. Johnson is dead. The thing is absurd on the face of it. There is room for some disagreement as to his position as a poet. On that question of poetry unanimity is ever hard to seek; so many mistake rhetoric for poetry. Only twice at the most, it seems to me, does Dr. Johnson reach anything in the shape of real inspiration in his many poems, {15} although it must be admitted that earlier generations admired them greatly. To have been praised ardently by Sir Walter Scott, by Byron, and by Tennyson should seem sufficient to demonstrate that he was a poet, were it not that, as I could prove if time allowed, poets are almost invariably bad critics of poetry. Sir Walter Scott read *The Vanity of Human Wishes* with "a choking sensation in the throat," and declared that he had more pleasure in reading that and Johnson's other long poem, *London*, than any other poetic compositions he could mention. But then I think it was always the sentiment in verse, and not its quality, that attracted Scott. Byron also declared that *The Vanity of Human Wishes* was "a great poem." Certainly these poems are quotable poems. Who does not recall the line about "surveying mankind from China to Peru," or think, as Johnson taught us, to:—

> Mark what ills the scholar's life assail,
> Toil, envy, want, the patron, and the jail.

Or remember his epitaph on one who:—

> Left a name at which the world grew pale,
> To point a moral or adorn a tale.

One line—"Superfluous lags the veteran on the stage" has done duty again and again. I might quote a hundred such examples to show Johnson, whatever his qualities as a poet, is very much alive indeed in his verse. It is, however, as a great prose writer, that I prefer to consider him. Here he is certainly one of the most permanent forces in our literature. *Rasselas*, for example, while never ranking with us moderns quite so high as it did with the excellent Miss Jenkins in *Cranford*, is a never failing delight. So far from being a dead book, is there a young man or a young woman setting out in the world of to-day, aspiring to an all-round literary cultivation, who is not required to know it? It has been republished continually. What novelist of our time would not give much to have so splendid a public recognition as was provided when Lord Beaconsfield, then Mr. Disraeli, after the Abyssinian Expedition, pictured in the House of Commons "the elephants of Asia dragging the artillery of Europe over the mountains of Rasselas."

Equally in evidence are those wonderful *Lives of The Poets* which Johnson did not complete until he was seventy-two years of age, literary efforts which have always seemed to me to be an encouraging demonstration that we should never allow ourselves to grow old. Many of these 'Lives' are very beautiful. They are all suggestive. Only the other day I read them again in the fine new edition that was prepared by that staunch Johnsonian, Dr. Birkbeck Hill. The greatest English critic of these latter days, Mr. Matthew Arnold, showed his appreciation by making a selection from them for popular use. From age to age every man with the smallest profession of interest in literature will study them. Of how many books can this be said?

Greatest of all was Johnson as a writer in his least premeditated work, his *Prayers and Meditations*. They take rank in my mind with the very best things of their kind, *The Meditations of Marcus Aurelius*, *The Confessions of Rousseau*, and similar books. They are healthier than any of their rivals. William Cowper, that always fascinating poet and beautiful letter writer, more than once disparaged Johnson in this connexion. Cowper said that he would like to have "dusted Johnson's jacket until his pension rattled in his pocket," for what he had said about Milton. He read some extracts, after Johnson's death, from the *Meditations*, and wrote contemptuously of them. {18} But if Cowper had always possessed, in addition to his fascinating other-worldliness the healthy worldliness of Dr. Johnson, perhaps we should all have been the happier. To me that collection of *Prayers and Meditations* seems one of the most helpful books that I have ever read, and I am surprised that it is not constantly reprinted in a handy form. {19} It is a valuable inspiration to men to keep up their spirits under adverse conditions, to conquer the weaknesses of their natures; not in the stifling manner of Thomas a Kempis, but in a breezy, robust way. Yes, I think that these three works, *Rasselas*, *The Lives of the Poets*, and the *Prayers and Meditations*, make it quite clear that Johnson still holds his place as one of our greatest writers, even if we were not familiar with his many delightful letters, and had not read his *Rambler*— which his old enemy, Miss Anna Seward, insisted was far better than Addison's *Spectator*.

All this is only to say that we cannot have too much of Dr. Johnson. The advantage of such a gathering as this is that it helps us to keep that fact alive. Moreover, I feel that it is a good thing if we can hearten those who have devoted themselves to laborious research connected with such matters. Take, for example, the work of Dr. Birkbeck Hill: his many volumes are a delight to the Johnson student. I knew Dr. Hill very well, and I have often felt that his work did not receive half the encouragement that it deserved. We hear sometimes, at least in London, of authors who advertise themselves. I rather fancy that all such advertisement is monopolized by the novelist, and that the newspapers do not trouble themselves very much about literary men who work in other fields than that of fiction. Fiction has much to be said for it, but as a rule it reaps its reward very promptly, both in finance and in fame. No such rewards come to the writer of biography, to the writer of history, to the literary editor. Dr. Hill's beautiful edition of Boswell's *Life*, with all its fascinating annotation, did not reach a second edition in his lifetime. I am afraid that the sum that he made out of it, or that his publishers made out of it, would seem a very poor reward indeed when gauged by the results in other fields of labour.

Within the past few weeks I have had the privilege of reading a book that continues these researches. Mr. Aleyn Lyell Reade has published a handsome tome, which he has privately printed, entitled *Dr. Johnson's Ancestry: His Kinsfolk and Family Connexions*. I am glad to hear that the Johnson Museum has purchased a copy, for such a work deserves every encouragement. The author must have spent hundreds of pounds, without the faintest possibility of obtaining either fame or money from the transaction. He seems to have employed copyists in every town in

Clement Shorter

Staffordshire, to copy wills, registers of births and deaths, and kindred records from the past. Now Dr. Birkbeck Hill could not have afforded to do this; he was by no means a rich man. Mr. Reade has clearly been able to spare no expense, with the result that here are many interesting facts corrective of earlier students. The whole is a valuable record of the ancestry of Dr. Johnson. It shows clearly that whereas Dr. Johnson thought very little of his ancestry, and scarcely knew anything of his grandfather on the paternal or the maternal side, he really sprang from a very remarkable stock, notably on the maternal side; and that his mother's family, the Fords, had among their connexions all kinds of fairly prosperous people, clergymen, officials, professional men as well as sturdy yeomen. These ancestors of Dr. Johnson did not help him much to push his way in the world. Of some of them he had scarcely heard. All the same it is of great interest to us to know this; it in a manner explains him. That before Samuel Johnson was born, one of his family had been Lord Mayor of London, another a Sheriff, that they had been associated in various ways, not only with the city of his birth, but also with the great city which Johnson came to love so much, is to let in a flood of fresh light upon our hero. My time does not permit me to do more than make a passing reference to this book, but I should like to offer here a word of thanks to its author for his marvellous industry, and a word of congratulation to him for the extraordinary success that has accrued to his researches.

I mention Mr. Reade's book because it is full of Lichfield names and Lichfield associations, and it is with Dr. Johnson's life-long connexion with Lichfield that all of us are thinking to-night. Now here I may say, without any danger of being challenged by some visitor who has the misfortune not to be a citizen of Lichfield—you who are will not wish to challenge me—that this city has distinguished itself in quite an unique way. I do not believe that it can be found that any other town or city of England—I will not say of Scotland or of Ireland—has done honour to a literary son in the same substantial measure that Lichfield has done honour to Samuel Johnson. The peculiar glory of the deed is that it was done to the living Johnson, not coming, as so many honours do, too late for a man to find pleasure in the recognition. We know that—

Seven wealthy towns contend for Homer dead,
Through which the living Homer begged his bread.

But I doubt whether in the whole history of literature in England it can be found that any other purely literary man has received in his lifetime so substantial a mark of esteem from the city which gave him birth, as Johnson did when your Corporation, in 1767, "at a common-hall of the bailiffs and citizens, without any solicitation," presented him with the ninety-nine years' lease of the house in which he was born. Your citizens not only did that for Johnson, but they gave him other marks of their esteem. He writes from Lichfield to Sir Joshua Reynolds to express his pleasure that his portrait has been "much visited and much admired." "Every man," he adds, "has a lurking desire to appear considerable in his native place." Then we all remember Boswell's naive confession that his pleasure at finding his hero so much beloved led him, when the pair arrived at this very hostelry, to imbibe too much of the famous Lichfield ale. If Boswell wished, as he says, to offer incense to the spirit of the place, how much more may we desire to do so to-night, when exactly 125 years have passed, and his hero is now more than ever recognized as a king of men.

I do not suggest that we should honour Johnson in quite the same way that Boswell did. This is a more abstemious age. But we must drink to his memory all the same. Think of it. A century and a quarter have passed since that memorable evening at the *Three Crowns*, when Johnson and Boswell thus foregathered in this very room. You recall the journey from Birmingham of the two companions. "We are getting out of a state of death," the Doctor said with relief, as he approached his native city, feeling all the magic and invigoration that is said to come to those who in later years return to "calf-land." Then how good he was to an old schoolfellow who called upon him here. The fact that this man had failed in the battle of life while Johnson had succeeded, only made the Doctor the kinder. I know of no more human picture than that—"A Mr. Jackson," as he is called by Boswell, "in his coarse grey coat," obviously very poor, and as Boswell suggests, "dull and untaught." The "great Cham of Literature" listens patiently as the worthy Jackson tells his troubles, so much more patiently than he would have listened to one of the famous men of his Club in London, and the hero-worshipping Boswell drinks his deep potations, but never neglects to take notes the while. Of Boswell one remembers further that Johnson had told Wilkes that he had brought him to Lichfield, "my native city," "that he might see for once real Civility—for you know he lives among savages in Scotland, and among rakes in London." All good stories are worth hearing again and again, and so I offer an apology for recalling the picture to your mind at this time and in this place.

Alas! I have not the gift of the worldfamed Lord Verulam, who, as Francis Bacon, sat in the House of Commons. The members, we are told, so delighted in his oratory that when he rose to speak they "were fearful lest he should make an end." I am making an end. Johnson then was not only a great writer, a conversationalist so unique that his sayings have passed more into current speech than those of any other Englishman, but he was also a great moralist—a superb inspiration to a better life. We should not love Johnson so much were he not presented to us as a man of many weaknesses and faults akin to our own, not a saint by any means, and therefore not so far removed from us as some more ethereal characters of whom we may read. Johnson striving to methodize his life, to fight against sloth and all the minor vices to which he was prone, is the Johnson whom some of us prefer to keep ever in mind. "Here was," I quote Carlyle, "a strong and noble man, one of our great English souls." I love him best in his book called *Prayers and Meditations*, where we know him as we know scarcely any other Englishman, for the good, upright fighter in this by no means easy battle of life. It is as such a fighter that we think of him to-night. Reading the account of *his* battles may help us to fight ours.

Gentlemen, I give you the toast of the evening. Let us drink in solemn silence, upstanding, "The Immortal Memory of Dr. Samuel Johnson."

Clement Shorter

II

TO THE IMMORTAL MEMORY OF
WILLIAM COWPER

An address entitled 'The Sanity of Cowper,' delivered at the Centenary Celebration at Olney, Bucks, on the occasion of the Hundredth Anniversary of the Death of the poet William Cowper, April 25, 1900.

I owe some apology for coming down to Olney to take part in what I believe is a purely local celebration, in which no other Londoner, as far as I know, has been asked to take part. I am here not because I profess any special qualification to speak about Cowper, in the town with which his name is so pleasantly associated, but because Mr. Mackay, {31} the son-in-law of your Vicar, has written a book about the Brontes, and I have done likewise, and he asked me to come. This common interest has little, you will say, to do with the Poet of Olney. Between Cowper and Charlotte Bronte there were, however, not a few points of likeness or at least of contrast. Both were the children of country clergymen; both lived lives of singular and, indeed, unusual strenuousness; both were the very epitome of a strong Protestantism; and yet both—such is the inevitable toleration of genius—were drawn in an unusual manner to attachment to friends of the Roman Catholic Church—Cowper to Lady Throckmorton, who copied out some of his translations from Homer for him, assisted by her father-confessor, Dr. Gregson, and Miss Bronte to her Professor, M. Heger, the man in the whole world whom she most revered. Under circumstances of peculiar depression both these great Protestant writers went further on occasion than their Protestant friends would have approved, Cowper to contemplate—so he assures us in one of his letters—the entering a French monastery, and Miss Bronte actually to kneel in the Confessional in a Brussels church. Further, let me remind you that there were moments in the lives of Charlotte Bronte and her sisters, when Cowper's poem, *The Castaway*, was their most soul-stirring reading. Then, again, Mary Unwin's only daughter became the wife of a Vicar of Dewsbury, and it was at Dewsbury and to the very next vicar, that Mr. Bronte, the father of Charlotte, was curate when he first went into Yorkshire. Finally, let it be recalled that Cowper and Charlotte Bronte have attracted as much attention by the pathos of their lives as by anything that they wrote. Thus far, and no further, can a strained analogy carry us. The most enthusiastic admirers of the Brontes can only claim for them that they permanently added certain artistic treasures to our literature. Cowper did incomparably more than this. His work marked an epoch.

But first let me say how interested we who are strangers naturally feel in being in Olney. To every lover of literature Olney is made classic ground by the fact that Cowper spent some twenty years of his life in it—not always with too genial a contemplation of the place and its inhabitants. "The genius of Cowper throws a halo of glory over all the surroundings of Olney and Weston," says Dean Burgon. But Olney has claims apart from Cowper. John Newton {34} presents himself to me as an impressive personality. There was a time, indeed, of youthful impetuosity when I positively hated him, for Southey, whose biography I read very early in life, certainly endeavours to assist the view that Newton was

Clement Shorter

largely responsible for the poet's periodical attacks of insanity.

But a careful survey of the facts modifies any such impression. Newton was narrow at times, he was over-concerned as to the letter, often ignoring the spirit of true piety, but the student of the two volumes of his *Life and Correspondence* that we owe to Josiah Bull, will be compelled to look at "the old African blasphemer" as he called himself, with much of sympathy. That he had a note of tolerance, with which he is not usually credited, we learn from one of his letters, where he says:

I am willing to be a debtor to the wise and to the unwise, to doctors and shoemakers, if I can get a hint from any one without respect of parties. When a house is on fire Churchmen and Dissenters, Methodists and Papists, Moravians and Mystics are all welcome to bring water. At such times nobody asks, "Pray, friend, whom do you hear?" or "What do you think of the five points?"

Even my good friend Canon Benham, who has done so much to sustain the honourable fame of Cowper, and who would have been here to-day but for a long-standing engagement, is scarcely fair to Newton. {35} It is not true, as has been suggested, that Cowper always changed his manner into one of painful sobriety when he wrote to Newton. One of his most humorous letters—a rhyming epistle—was addressed to that divine.

I have writ (he says) in a rhyming fit, what will make you dance, and as you advance, will keep you still, though against your will, dancing away, alert and gay, till you come to an end of what I have penned; which you may do ere Madam and you are quite worn out with jigging about, I take my leave, and here you receive a bow profound, down to the ground, from your humble me, W. C.

Now, I quote this very familiar passage from the correspondence to remind you that Cowper could only have written it to a man possessed of considerable healthy geniality.

At any rate, alike as a divine and as the author of the *Olney Hymns*, Newton holds an important place in the history of theology, and Olney has a right to be proud of him. An even more important place is held by Thomas Scott, {36} and it seems to me quite a wonderful thing that Olney should sometimes have held at one and the same moment three such remarkable men as Cowper, Newton, and Scott.

In my boyhood Scott's name was a household word, and many a time have I thumbed the volumes of his *Commentaries*, those *Commentaries* which Sir James Stephen declared to be "the greatest theological performance of our age and country." Of Scott Cardinal Newman in his *Apologia* said, it will be remembered, that "to him, humanly speaking, I almost owe my soul." Even here our literary associations with Olney and its neighbourhood are not ended, for, it was within five miles of this town—at Easton Maudit—that Bishop Percy {37} lived and prepared those *Reliques* which have inspired a century of ballad literature. Here the future Bishop of Dromore was visited by Dr. Johnson and others. What a pity that with only five miles separating them Cowper and Johnson should never have met! Would Cowper have reconsidered the wish made when he read Johnson's biography of Milton in the *Lives of the Poets*: "Oh! I could thresh his old jacket till I made his pension jingle in his pocket!"?

But it is with Cowper only that we have here to do, and when we are talking of Cowper the difficulty is solely one of compression. So much has been written about him and his work. The Lives of him form of themselves a most substantial library. He has been made the subject of what is surely the very worst biography in the language and of one that is among the very best. The well-meaning Hayley {38a} wrote the one, in which the word "tenderness" appears at least twice on every page, and Southey {38b} the other. Not less fortunate has the poet been in his critics. Walter Bagehot, James Russell Lowell, Mrs. Oliphant, George Eliot {38c}—these are but a few of the names that occur to me as having said something wise and to the point concerning the Poet of Olney.

I somehow feel that it is safer for me to refer to the Poet of Olney than to speak of William Cowper, because I am not quite sure how you would wish me to pronounce his name. *Cooper*, he himself pronounced it, as his family are in the habit of doing. The present Lord Cowper is known to all the world as Lord Cooper. The derivation of the name and the family coat-of-arms justify that pronunciation, and it might be said that a man was, and is, entitled to settle the question of the pronunciation of his own name. And yet I plead for what I am quite willing to allow is the incorrect pronunciation. All pronunciation, even of the simplest words, is settled finally by a consensus of custom. Throughout the English-speaking world the name is now constantly pronounced Cowper, as if that most useful and ornamental animal the cow had given it its origin. Well-read Scotland is peculiarly unanimous in the custom, and well-read America follows suit. William Shakspere, I doubt not, called himself Shaxspere, and we decline to imitate him, and so probably many of us will with a light heart go on speaking of William Cowper to the end of the chapter. At any rate Shakspere and Cowper, divergent as were their lives and their work—and one readily recognizes the incomparably greater position of the former—had alike a keen sense of humour, rare among poets it would seem, and hugely would they both have enjoyed such a controversy as this.

This suggestion of the humour of Cowper brings me to my main point. Humour is so essentially a note of sanity, and it is the sanity of Cowper that I desire to emphasize here. We have heard too much of the insanity of Cowper, of the "maniac's tongue" to which Mrs. Browning referred, of the "maniacal Calvinist" of whom Byron wrote somewhat scornfully. Only a day or two ago I read in a high-class journal that "one fears that Cowper's despondency and madness are better known to-day than his poetry." That is not to know the secret of Cowper. It is true that there were periods of maniacal depression, and these were not always religious ones. Now, it was from sheer nervousness at the prospect of meeting his fellows, now it was from a too logical acceptance of the doctrine of eternal punishment. Had it not been these, it would have been something else. It might have been politics, or a hundred things that now and again give a twist to the mind of the wisest. With Cowper it was generally religion. I am not here to promote a paradox. I accept the only too well-known story of Cowper's many visitations, but, looking back a century, for the purpose of asking what was Cowper's contribution to the world's happiness and why we meet to speak of our love for him to-day, I insist that these visitations are not essential to our memory of him as a great figure in our literature—the maker of an epoch.

Cowper lived for some seventy years—sixty-nine, to be exact. Of these years there was a period longer than the full term of Byron's life, of Shelley's or of Keats's, of perfect sanity, and it was in this period that he gave us what is one of the sanest achievements in our literature, view it as we may.

Let us look backwards over the century—a century which has seen many changes of which Cowper had scarcely any vision—the wonders of machinery and of electricity, of commercial enterprise, of the newspaper press, of book production. The galloping postboy is the most persistent figure in Cowper's landscape. He has been replaced by the motor car. Nations have arisen and fallen; a thousand writers have become popular and have ceased to be remembered. Other writers have sprung up who have made themselves immortal. Burns and Byron, Coleridge and Wordsworth, Scott and Shelley among the poets.

We ask ourselves, then, what distinctly differentiates Cowper's life from that of his brothers in poetry, and I reply—his sanity. He did not indulge in vulgar amours, as did Burns and Byron; he did not ruin his moral fibre by opium, as did Coleridge; he did not shock his best friends by an over-weening egotism, as did Wordsworth; he did not spoil his life by reckless financial complications, as did Scott; or by too great an enthusiasm to beat down the world's conventions, as did Shelley. I do not here condemn any one or other of these later poets. Their lives cannot be summed up in the mistakes they made. I only urge that, as it is not good to be at warfare with your fellows, to be burdened with debts that you have to kill yourself to pay, to alienate your friends by distressing mannerisms, to cease to be on speaking terms with your family—therefore Cowper, who avoided these things, and, out of threescore years and more allotted to him, lived for some forty or fifty years at least a quiet, idyllic life, surrounded by loyal and loving friends, had chosen the saner and safer path. That, it may be granted, was very much a matter of temperament, and for it one does not need to praise him. The appeal to us of Robert Burns to gently scan our brother man will necessarily find a ready acceptance to-day, and a plea on behalf of kindly toleration for any great writer who has inspired his fellows is natural and honourable. But Cowper does not require any such kindly toleration. His temperament led him to a placid life, where there were few temptations, and that life with its quiet walks, its occasional drives, its simple recreations, has stood for a whole century as our English ideal. It is what, amid the strain of the severest commercialism in our great cities, we look forward to for our declining years as a haven on this side of the grave.

But I have undertaken to plead for Cowper's sanity. I desire, therefore, to beg you to look not at this or that episode in his life, when, as we know, Cowper was in the clutches of evil spirits, but at his life as a whole—a life of serene content-ment in the company of his friends, his hares Puss, Tiny and Bess, his "eight pair of tame pigeons," his correspondents; and then I ask you to turn to his work, and to note the essential sanity of that work also.

First there is his poetry. When after the Bastille had fallen Charles James Fox quoted in one of his speeches Cowper's lines—written long years before—praying that that event might occur, he paid an unconscious tribute to the sanity of Cowper's genius. {44} Few poets who have let their convictions and aspirations find expression in verse have come so near the mark.

Wordsworth's verse—that which was written at the same age—is studded with prophecy of evils that never occurred. It was not because of any supermundane intelligence, such as latter-day poets have been pleased to affect and latter-day critics to assume for them, that Cowper wrote in anticipation of the fall of the Bastille in those thrilling lines, but because his exceedingly sane outlook upon the world showed him that France was riding fast towards revolution.

We have been told that Cowper's poetry lacked the true note of passion, that there was an absence of the "lyric cry." I protest that I find the note of passion in the "Lines on the

Receipt of my Mother's Picture," in his two sets of verses to Mrs. Unwin, in his sonnet to Wilberforce not less marked than I find it in other great poets. I find in *The Task* and elsewhere in Cowper's works a note of enthusiasm for human brotherhood, for man's responsibility for man, for universal kinship, that had scarcely any place in literature before he wrote quietly here at Olney thoughts wiser and saner than he knew. To-day we call ourselves by many names, Conservatives or Liberals, Radicals, or Socialists; we differ widely as to ways and means; but we are all practically agreed about one thing—that the art of politics is the art of making the world happier. Each politician who has any aspirations beyond mere ambition desires to leave the world a little better than he found it. This is a commonplace of to-day. It was not a commonplace of Cowper's day. Even the great-hearted, lovable Dr. Johnson was only concerned with the passing act of kindliness to his fellows; patriotism he declared to be the last refuge of a scoundrel; collective aspiration was mere charlatanry in his eyes, and when some one said that he had lost his appetite because of a British defeat, Johnson thought him an impostor, in which Johnson was probably right. There have been plenty of so-called patriots who were scoundrels, there has been plenty of affectation of sentiment which is little better than charlatanry, but we do not consider when we weigh the influence of men whether Rousseau was morally far inferior to Johnson. We know that he was. But Rousseau, poor an instrument as he may have been, helped to break many a chain, to relieve many a weary heart, to bring to whole peoples a new era in which the horrors of the past became as a nightmare, and in which ideals were destined to reign for ever. Cowper, an incomparably better man than Rousseau, helped to permeate England with that collective sentiment, which, while it does not excuse us for neglecting our neighbour, is a good thing for preserving for nations a healthy natural life, a more and more difficult task with the growing complications of commercialism. Cowper here, as I say, unconsciously performed his greatest service to humanity; and it was performed, be it remembered, at Olney. It has been truly said that in Cowper:—

> The poetry of human wrong begins, that long, long cry against oppression and evil done by man to man, against the political, moral, or priestly tyrant, which rings louder and louder through Burns, Coleridge, Shelley, and Byron, ever impassioned, ever longing, ever prophetic—never, in the darkest time, quite despairing. {47}

And Cowper achieved this without losing sight for one moment of the essential necessity for personal worth:

> Spend all thy powers
> Of rant and rhapsody in Virtue's praise,
> Be most sublimely good, verbosely grand,

and it profiteth nothing, he said in effect.

That was not his only service as a citizen. He struck the note of honest patriotism as it had not been struck before since Milton, by the familiar lines commencing:

> England, with all thy faults, I love thee still,
> My country!

As also in that stirring ballad "On the Loss of the *Royal George*:"

> Her timbers yet are sound,
> And she may float again,
> Full charged with England's thunder,
> And plough the distant main.

There are two other great claims that might here be made for Cowper did time allow, that he anticipated Wordsworth alike as a lover of nature, as one who had more than a superficial affection for it—the superficial affection of Thomson and Gray—and that he anticipated Wordsworth also as a lover of animal life. Cowper's love of nature was the less effective than Wordsworth's only, surely, in that he had not had Wordsworth's advantage of living amid impressive scenery. His love of animal life was far less platonic than Wordsworth's. To his hares and his pigeons and all dumb creatures he was genuinely devoted. Perhaps it was because he had in him the blood of kings—for, curiously enough, it is no more difficult to trace the genealogical tree of both Cowper and Byron down to William the Conqueror than it is to trace the genealogical tree of Queen Victoria—it was perhaps, I say, this descent from kings which led him to be more tolerant of "sport" than was Wordsworth. At any rate, Cowper's vigorous description of being in at the death of a fox may be contrasted with Wordsworth's "Heart Leap Well," and you will prefer Cowper or Wordsworth, as your tastes are for or against our old-fashioned English sports. But even then, as often, Cowper in his poetry was less tolerant than in his prose, for he writes in *The Task* of:

detested sport
That owes its pleasures to another's pain,

We may note in all this the almost entire lack of indebtedness in Cowper to his predecessors. One of his most famous phrases, indeed, that on "the cup that cheers, but not inebriates," he borrowed from Berkeley; but his borrowings were few, far fewer than those of any other great poet, whereas mine would be a long essay were I to produce by the medium of parallel columns all that other poets have borrowed from him.

Lastly, among Cowper's many excellencies as a poet let me note his humour. His pathos, his humanity—many fine qualities he has in common with others; but what shall we say of his humour? If the ubiquitous Scot were present, so far from his native heath—and I daresay we have one or two with us—he might claim that humour was also the prerogative of Robert Burns. He might claim, also, that certain other great characteristics of Cowper were to be found almost simultaneously in Burns. There is virtue in the almost. Cowper was born in 1731, Burns in 1759. At any rate humour has been a rare product among the greater English poets. It was entirely absent in Wordsworth, in Shelley, in Keats. Byron possessed a gift of satire and wit, but no humour, Tennyson only a suspicion of it in "The Northern Farmer." From Cowper to Browning, who also had it at times, there has been little humour in the greatest English poetry, although plenty of it in the lesser poets— Hood and the rest. But there was in Cowper a great sense of humour, as there was also plenty of what Hazlitt, almost censoriously, calls "elegant trifling." Not only in the imperishable "John Gilpin," but in the "Case Between Nose and Eyes," "The Nightingale and Glow-worm," and other pieces you have examples of humorous verse which will live as long as our language endures.

Cowper's claims as a poet, then, may be emphasized under four heads:—

I. His enthusiasm for humanity.

II. His love of nature.

III. His love of animal life.

IV. His humour.

And in three of these, let it be said emphatically, he stands out as the creator of a new era.

There is another claim I make for him, and with this I close—his position as a master of prose, as well as of poetry. Cowper was the greatest letter-writer in a language which has produced many great letter- writers—Walpole, Gray, Byron, Scott, FitzGerald, and a long list. But nearly all these men were men of affairs, of action. Given a good literary style they could hardly have been other than interesting, they had so much to say that they gained from external sources. Even FitzGerald—the one recluse—had all the treasures of literature constantly passing into his study. Cowper had but eighteen books altogether during many of his years in Olney, and some of us who have lent our volumes in the past and are still sighing over gaps in our shelves find consolation in the fact that six of Cowper's books had been returned to him after a friend had borrowed for twenty years or so. Now, it is comparatively easy to write good letters with a library around you; it is marvellous that Cowper could have done this with so little material, and his letters are, from this point of view, the best of all—"divine chit-chat" Coleridge called them. His simple style captivates us. And here let me say— keeping to my text—that it is the *sanest* of styles, a style with no redundancies, no rhetoric, no straining after effect. The outlook on life is sane—what could be finer than the chase for the lost hare, or the call of the Parliamentary candidate, or the flogging of the thief?—and the outlook on literature is particularly sane.

Cowper was well-nigh the only true poet in the first rank in English literature who was at the same time a true critic. Literary history affords a singular revelation of the wild and incoherent judgments of their fellows on the part of the poets. For praise or blame, there are few literary judgments of Byron, of Shelley, of Wordsworth that will stand.

Coleridge was a critic first, and his poetry, though good, is small in quantity, and the same may be said of Matthew Arnold. Tennyson discreetly kept away from prose, and his letters, be it remembered, lack distinction as do most letters of the nineteenth century. If, however, as we are really to believe, he it was who really made the first edition of Palgrave's *Golden Treasury of Lyric Poetry*, he came near to Cowper in his sanity of judgment, and one delights to think that in that precious volume Cowper ranks third—that is, after Shakspere and Wordsworth—in the number of selections that are there given, and rightly given, as imperishable masterpieces of English poetry. Tennyson, also, was at one with Cowper in declaring that an appreciation of *Lycidas* was a touchstone of taste for poetry. To Tennyson, as to Cowper, Milton was the one great English poet after Shakspere; and here, also, we revere the saneness of view. More sane too, was Cowper than any of the modern critics, in that he did not believe that mere technique was the standpoint from which all poetry must ultimately be judged.

"Give me," he says, "a manly rough line with a deal of meaning in it, rather than a whole poem full of musical periods, that have nothing in them, only smoothness to recommend them!"

And thus he justified Robert Browning and many another singer.

Let us then dismiss from our minds the one-sided picture of Cowper as a gloomy fanatic, who was always asking himself in Carlylian phrase, "Am I saved? Am I damned?" Let us remember him as staunch to the friends of his youth, sympathetic to his old schoolfellow, Warren Hastings, when the world would make him out too black. Opposed in theory to tobacco, how he delighted to welcome his good friend Mr. Bull. "My greenhouse," he says, "wants only the flavour of your pipe to make it perfectly delightful!" Naturally tolerant of total abstinence, he asks one friend to drink to the success of his Homer, and thanks another for a present of bottle-stands. From beginning to end, save in those periods of aberration, there is no more resemblance to Cowper in the picture that certain narrow-minded people have desired to portray than there is in these same people's conception of Martin Luther. The real Luther, who loved dancing and mirth and the joy of living as much as did any of the men he so courageously opposed, was not more remote from a conception of him once current in this country than was the real Cowper—the frank, genial humorist, who wrote "John Gilpin," who in his youth "giggled and made giggle" with his girl-cousins, and in his maturer years "laughed and made laugh" with Lady Austen and Lady Hesketh.

To all men there are periods of weariness and depression, side by side with periods of happiness and hopefulness. Cowper, alas! had more than his share of the tragedy of life, but let us not forget that he had some of its joy, and that joy is reflected for us in a substantial literary achievement, which has lived, and influenced the world, while his more tragic experiences may well be buried in oblivion. This, you may have noted, is not a criticism of Cowper, but an eulogy. I would wish to say, however, that the criticism of Cowper by living writers has been of surpassing excellence. For the first fifty or sixty years of the century that we are recalling Cowper was the most popular poet of our country, with Burns and Byron for rivals. He has been largely dethroned by Wordsworth and Shelley, and Tennyson, not one of whom has been praised too much. But if Cowper has sunk somewhat out of sight of late years, owing to inevitable circumstances, it is during these late years that he has secured the goodwill of the best living critics. Would that Mr. Leslie Stephen {56}—who wrote his life in the *Dictionary of National Biography*—would that Mr. Edmund

Gosse—who has so recently published a great biography of Cowper's memorable ancestor, Dr. Donne—were, one or other of them, here to-day; or Mr. Austin Dobson, who has visited Olney, and described his impressions; or Dr. Jessopp, who lives near Cowper's tomb in East Dereham Church. These writers are, alas! not with us, and some presentment of a poet they love has fallen to less capable hands.

But not the most brilliant of speeches, not all the enthusiasm of all the critics, can ever restore Cowper to his former immense popularity. We do well, however, to celebrate his centenary, because it is good at certain periods to remember our indebtedness to the great men who have helped us in literature or in life. But that is not to say that we work for the dethronement of later favourites. "Each age must write its own books," says Emerson, and this is particularly the case with the great body of poetry. Cowper, however, will live to all time among students of literature by his longer poems; he will live to all time among the multitude by his ballads and certain of his lyrics. He will, assuredly, live by his letters, to study which will be a thousand times more helpful to the young writer than many volumes of Addison, to whom we were once advised to devote our days and our nights. Cowper will live, above all, as a profoundly interesting and beautiful personality, as a great and good Englishman—the greatest of all the sons of this his adopted town.

III

TO THE IMMORTAL MEMORY OF
GEORGE BORROW

An Address delivered in Norwich on the Occasion of the Borrow Centenary, 1903.

One hundred years ago there was born some two miles from the pleasant little town of East Dereham, in this county, a child who was christened George Henry Borrow. That is why we are assembled here this evening. I count it one of the most interesting coincidences in literary history that only three years earlier there should have left the world in the same little town—a town only known perhaps to those of us who are Norfolk men—a poet who has always seemed to me to be one of the greatest glories of our literature: I mean William Cowper. Cowper died in April, 1800, and Borrow was born in July, 1803, in this same town of East Dereham: and there very much it might be thought, any point of likeness or of contrast must surely end.

Cowper and Borrow do, indeed, come into some trivial kind of kinship at one or two points. In reading Cowper's beautiful letters I have come across two addressed by him to one Richard Phillips, a bookseller of that day, who had been in prison for publishing some of Thomas Paine's works.

Cowper had been asked by Phillips to write a sympathetic poem denunciatory of the political and religious tyranny that had sent Phillips to jail. Cowper had at first agreed, but was afterwards advised not to have anything more to do with Phillips. Judging by the after career of Phillips, Cowper did wisely; for Phillips was not a good man, although twenty years later he had become a sheriff of London and was knighted. As Sir Richard Phillips he was visited by George Borrow, then a youth at the beginning of his career. Borrow came to Phillips armed with an introduction from William Taylor of Norwich, and his reception is most dramatically recorded in the pages of *Lavengro*. This is, however, to anticipate. Then there is a poem by Cowper to Sir John Fenn {62} the antiquary, the first editor of the famous *Paston Letters*. In it there is a reference to Fenn's spouse, who, under the pseudonym of "Mrs. Teachwell," wrote many books for children in her day. Now Borrow could remember this lady—Dame Eleanor Fenn—when he was a boy. He recalled the "Lady Bountiful leaning on her gold-headed cane, while the sleek old footman followed at a respectful distance behind." Lady Fenn was forty- six years old when Cowper referred to her. She was sixty-six when the boy Borrow saw her in Dereham streets. At no other points do these great East Dereham writers come upon common ground: Cowper during the greater part of his life was a recluse. He practically fled from the world. In reading the many letters he wrote—and they are among the best letters in the English language—one is struck by the small number of his correspondents. He had few acquaintances and still fewer friends. He had never seen a hill until he was sixty, and then it was only the modest hills of Sussex that seemed to him so supremely glorious. He was never on the Continent. For half a lifetime he did not move out of one county, the least picturesque part of Buckinghamshire, the neighbourhood of Olney and of Weston. There he wrote the poems that have been a delight to several generations, poems which although they may have gone out of fashion with many are still very dear to some among us; and there, as I have said, he wrote the incomparable letters that have an equally permanent place in literature.

You could not conceive a more extraordinary contrast than the life of this other writer associated with East Dereham, whom we have met to celebrate this evening. George Borrow was the son of a soldier, who had risen from the ranks, and of a mother who had been an actress. Soldier and actress both imply to all of us a restless, wandering life. The soldier was a Cornishman by birth, the actress was of French origin, and so you have blended in this little Norfolk boy—who is a Norfolk boy in spite of it all—every kind of nomadic habit, every kind of fiery, imaginative enthusiasm, a temperament not usually characteristic of those of us who claim East Anglia as the land of our birth or of our progenitors. I wish it were possible for me to reconstruct that Norwich world into which young George Borrow entered at thirteen years of age. That it was a Norwich of great intellectual activity is indisputable. In the year of Borrow's birth John Gurney, who died six years later, first became a partner in the Norwich bank. His more famous son, Joseph John Gurney—aged fifteen—left the Earlham home in order to study at Oxford. His sister, the still more famous Elizabeth Fry, was now twenty-three. So that when Borrow, the thirteen year old son of the veteran soldier—who had already been in Ireland picking up scraps of Irish, and in Scotland adding to his knowledge of Gaelic—settled down for some of his most impressionable years in Norwich, Joseph John Gurney was a young man of twenty-eight and Elizabeth Fry was thirty-six. Dr. James Martineau was eleven years of age and his sister Harriet was fourteen. Another equally clever woman, not then married to Austin, the famous jurist, was Sarah Taylor, aged twenty-three. This is but to name a few of the crowd of Norwich worthies of that day. Would that some one could produce a picture of the literary life of Norwich of this time and of a quarter of a century onward—a period that includes the famous Bishop Stanley's {66} occupancy of the See of Norwich and the visits to this city from all parts of England of a great number of famous literary men. It is my pleasant occupation to-night to endeavour to show that Borrow, the very least of these men and women in public estimation for a good portion of his life, and perhaps the least in popular judgment even since his death, was really the greatest, was really the man of all others to whom this beautiful city should do honour if it asks for a name out of its nineteenth century history to crown with local recognition.

For whatever homage may have fallen to Borrow during the half-century or more since his name first came upon many tongues Norwich, it must be admitted, has given very little of it. No one associated with your city, I repeat, but has heard of the Gurneys and the Martineaus, of the Stanleys and the Austins, whose life stories have made so large a part of your literary and intellectual history during this very period. But I turn in vain to a number of books that I have in my library for any information concerning one who is indisputably the greatest among the intellectual children of Norwich. I turn to Mr. Prothero's *Life of Dean Stanley*—not one word about Borrow; to that pleasant *Memoir* of Sarah Austin and her mother, Mrs. Taylor, called *Three Generations of a Norfolk Family*—again not one word. I turn to Mr. Braithwaite's biography of Joseph John Gurney, and to Mr. Augustus Hare's book *The Gurneys of Earlham*—upon these worthy biographers Borrow made no impression whatever, although Joseph John Gurney was personally helpful to him and we read in *Lavengro* of that pleasant meeting between the pair on the river bank when Mr. Gurney chided the boy Borrow or Lavengro for angling. "From that day," he says, "I became less and less a practitioner of that cruel fishing." In Harriet Martineau's *Autobiography*, which enjoyed its hour of fame when it was published twenty-six years ago, there is a contemptuous reference to the disciple of William Taylor, "this polyglot gentleman, who went through Spain disseminating Bibles." If Miss Martineau were alive now she would hear the works of "this polyglot gentleman" praised on every hand, and would find that a cult had arisen which to her would certainly be quite incomprehensible. In that large, dismal book—the *Life of James Martineau*, again, there is but one mention of Dr. Martineau's famous schoolfellow whose name has been linked with him only by a silly story. Do not let it be thought that I am complaining of this neglect; the world will always treat its greatest writers in precisely this fashion. Borrow did not lack for fame of a kind, but he was, as I desire to show, praised in his lifetime for the wrong thing, where he was praised at all. Everyone in the fifties and sixties read *The Bible in Spain*, as they read a hundred other books of that period, now forgotten. Many read it who were deceived by its title. They expected a tract. Many read it as we to-day read the latest novel or biography of the hour. Then a new book arises and the momentary favourite is forgotten. We think for a whole week that we are in contact with a well-nigh immortal work. A little later we concern ourselves not at all whether the book is immortal or not. We go on to something else. The critic is as much to blame as the reader. Not one man in a hundred whose profession it is to come between the author and the public, and to guide the reader to the best in literature, has the least perception of what is good literature. It is easy when a writer has captured the suffrages of the crowd for the critic to tell the world that he is great. That happened to Carlyle, to Tennyson, to many a popular author whose earliest books commanded little attention: but, happily, these writers did not lose heart. They kept on writing. Borrow was otherwise made. He wrote *The Bible in Spain*—a book of travel of surprising merit. It sold largely on its title. Mr. Augustine Birrell has told us that he knew a boy in a very strict household who devoured the narrative on Sunday afternoons, the title being thought to cover a conventional missionary journey. Well, when I was a boy *The Bible in Spain* had gone out of fashion and the public had not taken up with the author's greater work, *Lavengro*. Borrow was naturally disappointed. He abused the critics and the public. Perhaps he grew somewhat soured. He did not hesitate in *The Romany Rye* to talk candidly about those "ill-favoured dogs . . . the newspaper editors," and he made the gentleman's gentleman of *Lavengro* describe how he was excluded from the Servants' Club in Park Lane because his master followed a profession "so mean as literature." In fact as a reaction from the unfriendly reception accorded to the *Romany Rye*—now one of the most costly of his books in a first edition—he lost heart, and he grew to despise the whole literary and writing class. Hence the various stories presenting him in not very sympathetic guise, the story of Thackeray being snubbed on asking Borrow if he had read the *Snob Papers*, of Miss Agnes Strickland receiving an even more forcible rebuff when she offered to send him her *Queens of England*. "For God's sake don't Madame; I should not know where to put them or what to do with them." These stories are in Gordon Hake's *Memoirs of Eighty Years*, but Mr. Francis Hindes Groome has shown us the other side of the picture, and others also to whom I shall refer a little later have done the same. Perhaps the literary class is never the worse for a little plain speaking. The real secret of Borrow is this—that he was a man of action turned into a writer by force of circumstances.

The life of Borrow, unlike that of most famous men of letters, has not been overwritten. His death in 1881 caused little emotion and attracted but small attention in the newspapers. *The Times*, then as now so excellent in its biographies as a rule, devoted but twenty lines to him. Here I may be pardoned for being autobiographical. I was last in Norwich in the early eighties. I had a wild enthusiasm for literature so far as my taste had been directed—that is to say I read every book I came across and had been doing so from my earliest boyhood. But I had never heard of George Borrow or of his works. In my then not infrequent visits to Norwich I cannot recall that his name was ever mentioned, and in my life in London, among men who were, many of them, great readers, I never heard of Borrow or of his achievement. He died in 1881, and as I do not recall hearing his name at the time of his death or until long afterwards, I must have missed certain articles in the *Athenaeum*—two of them admirable "appreciations" by Mr. Watts-Dunton—and so my state of benightedness was as I have described. It may be that those who are a year or two older than I am and those who are younger may find this extraordinary. You have always heard of Borrow and of his works, but I think I am entitled to insist that when Borrow sank into his grave, an old, and to many an eccentric and bitter man, he had fallen into the most curious oblivion with the public that has ever come to a man, I will not say of equal distinction, but of any distinction whatever. Mr. Egmont Hake told the readers of the *Athenaeum* in a biography that appeared at the time of Borrow's death that Borrow's works were "forgotten in England" and I find in turning to the biography of Borrow in *The Norvicensian*, for 1882—the organ of the Norwich Grammar School—that the writer of this obituary notice confessed that there were none of Borrow's works in the library of the school of which Borrow had been the most distinguished pupil.

From that time—in 1881—until 1899, a period of eighteen years, Borrow had but little biographical recognition. A few introductions to his books, sundry encyclopaedia articles, and one or two magazine essays made up the sum total of information concerning the author of *Lavengro* until Dr. Knapp's *Life* appeared in 1899. That *Life* has been severely handled by some lovers of Borrow, and lovers of Borrow are now plentiful enough. Dr. Knapp had not the cunning of the really successful biographer. His book still remains in the huge two-volumed form in which it was first issued four years ago, and I do not anticipate that it will ever be a popular book. There is no literary art in it. There is a capacity for amassing facts, but no power of co-ordinating these facts. Moreover Dr. Knapp did a great deal of mischief by very over-zeal. He made too great a research into all the current gossip in Norfolk and Suffolk concerning Borrow. If you were to make special research into the life of any friend or acquaintance of the past you would hear much foolish gossip and a great many wrong motives imputed, and possibly you would not have an opportunity of checking the various statements. The whole of Dr. Knapp's book seems to be written upon the principle of "I would if I could" say a good many things, and, indeed, every few months there appears in the *Eastern Daily Press*, a journal of your city that I have read every day regularly since boyhood, a letter from some one explaining that the less inquiry about this or that point in Borrow's career the better for Borrow. Take, for example, last Saturday's issue of the journal I have named, where I find the following from a correspondent:—

Dr. Knapp, from dictates of courtesy, left it unrevealed, and as he could say nothing to Borrow's credit, passed the affair over in silence, and on this point all well-wishers of Borrow's reputation would be wise to take their cue from this biographer's example.

Now there is nothing more damnatory than a sentence of this kind. What does it amount to? What is the 'it' that is unrevealed by the courteous Dr. Knapp? It seems to amount to the charge that Borrow is accused of gibbeting in his books the people he dislikes; this is what every great imaginative writer has been charged with to the perplexing of dull people. There are many characters in Dickens's novels which are supposed to be a presentation of near relatives or friends. These he ought to have treated with more kindliness. That heroic little woman, Miss Bronte, gave a picture of Madame Heger, who kept a school at Brussels, that conveyed, I doubt not, a very mistaken presentation of the subject of her satire. Imaginative writers have always taken these liberties. When the worst is said it simply amounts to this, that Borrow was a good hater. Dr. Johnson said that he loved a good hater, and he might very well have loved Borrow. Dante, whom we all now agree to idolize, treated people even more roughly; he placed some of his acquaintances who had ill-used him in the very lowest circles of hell. May I express a hope, therefore, that this type of letter to the Norwich newspapers about Dr. Knapp's "kindness" to Borrow's reputation may cease. If Dr. Knapp had printed the whole of the facts we should know how to deal with them; but this is one of his limitations as a biographer. He has not in the least helped to a determination of Borrow's real character.

Had Borrow possessed a biographer so skilful with her pen as Mrs. Gaskell in her *Life of Charlotte Bronte*, so keen-eyed for the dramatic note as Sir George Trevelyan in his *Life of Macaulay*, he would have multiplied readers for *Lavengro*. There are many people who have read the Bronte novels from sheer sympathy with the writers that their biographer, Mrs. Gaskell, had kindled. Let us not, however, be ungrateful to Dr. Knapp. He has furnished those of us who are sufficiently interested in the subject with a fine collection of documents. Here is all the material of biography in its crude state, but presenting vividly enough the live Borrow to those who have the perception to read it with care and judgment. Still more grateful may we be to Dr. Knapp for his edition of Borrow's works, particularly for those wonderful episodes in *Lavengro* which he has reproduced from the original manuscript, episodes as dramatic as any other portion of the text, and making Dr. Knapp's edition of *Lavengro* the only possible one to possess.

But to return to the main facts of Borrow's career, which every one here at least is familiar with. You know of his birth at East Dereham, of his life in Ireland and in Scotland, of his school days at Norwich, of his departure from Norwich to London on his father's death, of his dire struggles in the literary whirlpool, and of his wanderings in gipsy land. You know, thanks to Dr. Knapp, more than you could otherwise have learned of his life at St. Petersburg, whither he had been sent by the Bible Society, on the recommendation of Mr. Joseph John Gurney and another patron. Then he has himself told us in picturesque fashion of his life in Portugal and Spain. After this we hear of his marriage to Mary Clarke, his residence from 1840 to 1853 at Oulton, in Suffolk, from 1853 to 1860 at Yarmouth, from 1860 to 1874 in Hereford Square, London, and finally from 1874 to 1881 at Oulton, where he died. That is the bare skeleton of Borrow's life, and for half his life, I think, we should be content with a skeleton. For the other half of it we have the best autobiography in the English language. An autobiography that ranks with Goethe's *Truth and Poetry from my Life* and Rousseau's *Confessions*. In four books—in *Lavengro*, *Romany Rye*, *The Bible in Spain*, and *Wild Wales* we have some delightful glimpses of an interesting personality, and here we may leave the personal side of Borrow. Beyond this we know that he was unquestionably a devoted son, a good husband, a kind father. The literary life has its perils, so far as domesticity is concerned. Sir Walter Scott in his life of Dryden speaks of:—

Her who had to endure the apparently causeless fluctuation of spirits incidental to one compelled to dwell for long periods of time in the fitful realms of the imagination, and it is certain that those who dwell in the realms of the imagination are usually very irritable, very difficult to live with. Literary history in its personal side is largely a dismal narrative of the uncomfortable relations of men of genius with their wives and with their families. Your man of genius thinks himself bound to hang up his fiddle in his own house, however merry a fellow he may prove himself to a hundred boon companions outside. George Borrow was perhaps the opposite of all this. As a companion and a neighbour he did not always shine, if the impression of many a witness is to be trusted. They tell anecdotes of his lack of cordiality, of his unsociability, and so on. They have told those anecdotes more industriously in Norwich than anywhere else. He himself in an incomparable account of going to church with the gypsies in *The Romany Rye* has the following:

It appeared as if I had fallen asleep in the pew of the old church of pretty Dereham. I had occasionally done so when a child, and had suddenly woke up. Yes, surely, I had been asleep and had woke up; but no! if I had been asleep I had been waking in my sleep, struggling, striving, learning and unlearning in my sleep. Years had rolled away whilst I had been asleep—ripe fruit had fallen, green fruit had come on whilst I had been asleep—how circumstances had altered, and above all myself whilst I had been asleep. No, I had not been asleep in the old church! I was in a pew, it is true, but not the pew of black leather, in which I sometimes fell asleep in days of yore, but in a strange pew; and then my companions, they were no longer those of days of yore. I was no longer with my respectable father and mother, and my dear brother, but with the gypsy cral and his wife, and the gigantic Tawno, the Antinous of the dusky people. And what was I myself? No longer an innocent child but a moody man, bearing in my face, as I knew well, the marks of my strivings and strugglings; of what I had learnt and unlearnt.

But this "moody man," let it be always remembered, was a good husband and father. His wife was devoted to him, his step-daughter carries now to an old age a profound reverence and affection for his memory. Grieved beyond all words was she—the Henrietta or "Hen" of all his books—at what is maintained to be the utterly fictitious narrative of Borrow's described deathbed that Professor Knapp presented from the ill-considered gossip that he picked up while staying in the neighbourhood. {80} Borrow has himself something to say concerning his family in *Wild Wales*:—

> Of my wife I will merely say that she is a perfect paragon of wives—can make puddings and sweets and treacle posset, and is the best woman of business in East Anglia: of my step-daughter, for such she is though I generally call her daughter, and with good reason seeing that she has always shown herself a daughter to me, that she has all kinds of good qualities and several accomplishments, knowing something of conchology, more of botany, drawing capitally in the Dutch style, and playing remarkably well on the guitar.

Yes, I am not quite sure but that Borrow was really a good fellow all round, as well as being a good husband and father. He hated the literary class, it is true. He considered that the "contemptible trade of author," as he called it, was less creditable than that of a jockey. He avoided as much as possible the writers of books, and particularly the blue-stocking, and when they came in his way he was not always very polite, sometimes much the reverse. Only the other day a letter was published from the late Professor Cowell describing a visit to Borrow and his not very friendly reception. Well, Borrow was here as elsewhere a man of insight. The literary class is usually a very narrow class. It can talk about no trade but its own. Things have grown worse since Borrow's day, I am sure, but they were bad enough then. Borrow was a man of very varied tastes. He took interest in gypsies and horses and prize fighters and a hundred other entertaining matters, and so he despised the literary class, which cared for none of these things. But unhappily for his fame the literary class has had the final word; it has revealed all the gossip of a gossiping peasantry, and it has done its best to present the recluse of Oulton in a disagreeable light. Fortunately for Borrow, who kept the bores at bay and contented himself with but few friends, there were at least two who survived him to bear testimony to the effect that he was "a singularly steadfast and loyal friend." One of these was Mr. Watts-Dunton, who tells us in one of his essays that:

> George Borrow was a good man, a most winsome and a most charming companion, an English gentleman, straightforward, honest, and brave as the very best exemplars of that fine old type.

I have dwelt longer on this aspect of my subject than I should have done had I been addressing any other audience than a Norwich one. But the fact is that all the gossip and backbiting and censoriousness that has gathered round Borrow for a hundred years has come out of this very city, commencing with the "bursts of laughter" that, according to Miss Martineau, greeted Borrow's travels in Spain for the Bible Society. Borrow was twenty-one years of age when he left Norwich to make his way in the world. During the next twenty years he may have undergone many changes of intellectual view, as most of us do, as Miss Martineau notably did, and Miss Martineau and her laughing friends were diabolically uncharitable. That lack of charity followed Borrow throughout his life. He was libelled by many, by Miss Frances Power Cobbe most of all. However, the great city of Norwich will make up for it in the future, and she will love Borrow as Borrow indisputably loved her. How he praised her fine cathedral, her lordly castle, her Mousehold Heath, her meadows in which he once saw a prize fight, her pleasant scenery—no city, not even glorious Oxford, has been so well and adequately praised, and I desire to show that that praise is not for an age but for all time.

If George Borrow has not been happy in his biographer, and if, as is true, he has received but inadequate treatment on this account—such series of little books as *The English Men of Letters* and the *Great Writers* quite ignoring him—he has been equally unfortunate in his critics. There are hardly any good and distinctive appreciations in print of Borrow's works. While other great names in the great literature of the Victorian Period have been praised by a hundred pens, there has scarcely been any notable and worthy praise of Borrow, and if I were in an audience that was at all sceptical as to Borrow's supreme merits, which happily I am not; if I were among those who declared that they could see but small merit in Borrow themselves, but were prepared to accept him if only I could bring good authority that he was a very great writer, I should be hardly put to to comply with the demand. I can only name Mr. Theodore Watts-Dunton and Mr. Augustine Birrell as critics of considerable status who have praised Borrow well. "The delightful, the bewitching, the never sufficiently-to-be-praised George Borrow," says Mr. Birrell in one of the essays he has written on the subject; {84} while Mr. Theodore Watts-Dunton, has written no less than four papers on one whom he knew and admires personally, and of whom he insists that "his idealizing powers, his romantic cast of mind, his force, his originality, give him a title to a permanent place high in the ranks of English prose writers."

All this is very interesting, but in literature as in life we have got to work out our own destinies. We have not got to accept Borrow because this or that critic tells us he is good. I have therefore no quarrel with any one present who does not share my view that Borrow was one of the greater glories of English literature. I only desire to state my case for him.

To be a lover of Borrow, a Borrovian, in fact, it is not necessary to know all his books. You may never have seen copies of the *Romantic Ballads* or of *Faustus*, of *Targum* or of *The Turkish Jester*, of Borrow's translation of *The Talisman* of Pushkin. Your state may be none the less gracious. To possess these books is largely a collector's hobby. They are interesting, but they would not have made for the author an undying reputation. Further, you may not care for *The Bible in Spain*, you may be untouched by the *Gypsies in Spain* and *Wild Wales*, and even then I will not deny to you the title of a good Borrovian, if only you pronounce *Lavengro* and *The Romany Rye* to be among the greatest books you know. I can admire the *Gypsies in Spain* and *Wild Wales*. I can read *The Bible in Spain* with something of the enthusiasm with which our fathers read it. It is a stirring narrative of travel and much more. Robert Louis Stevenson did, indeed, rank it among his "dear acquaintances" in bookland, "the *Pilgrim's Progress* in the first rank, *The Bible in Spain* not far behind," he says. All the same, it has not, none of these three books has, the distinctive mark of first class genius that belongs to the other two in the five-volumed edition of Borrow's Collected Works that many of us have read through more than once. Not all clever people have thought *Lavengro* and *The Romany Rye* to be thus great. A critic in the *Athenaeum* declared *Lavengro* when it was published in 1851 to be "balderdash," while a critic writing just fifty years afterwards and writing from Norfolk, alas! insisted that the author of this book "was absolutely wanting in the power of invention" that he (Borrow) could "only have drawn upon his memory," that he had "no sense of humour." If all this were true, if half of it were true, Borrow was not the great man, the great writer that I take him to be. But it is not true. *Lavengro* with its continuation *The Romany Rye*, is a great work of imagination, of invention; it is in no sense a photograph, a memory picture, and it abounds in humour as it abounds in many other great characteristics. What makes an author supremely great? Surely a certain quality which we call genius, as distinct from the mere intellectual power of some less brilliant writer:—

True genius is the ray that flings
A novel light o'er common things

and here it is that Borrow shines supreme. He has invested with quite novel light a hundred commonplace aspects of life. Not an inventor! not imaginative! Why, one of the indictments against him is that philologists decry his philology and gyptologists his gypsy learning. If, then, his philology and his gypsy lore were imperfect, as I believe they were, how much the greater an imaginative writer he was. To say that *Lavengro* merely indicates keen observation is absurd. Not the keenest observation will crowd so many adventures, adventures as fresh and as novel as those of Gil Blas or Robinson Crusoe, into a few months' experience. "I felt some desire," says Lavengro, "to meet with one of those adventures which upon the roads of England are generally as plentiful as blackberries in autumn." I think that most of us will wander along the roads of England for a very long time before we meet an Isopel Berners, before we have such an adventure as that of the blacksmith and his horse, or of the apple woman whose favourite reading was *Moll Flanders*. These and a hundred other adventures, the fight with the Flaming Tinman, the poisoning of Lavengro by the gypsy woman, the discourse with Ursula under the hedge, when once read are fixed upon the memory for ever. And yet you may turn to them again and again, and with ever increasing zest. The story of Isopel Berners is a piece of imaginative

Clement Shorter

writing that certainly has no superior in the literature of the last century. It was assuredly no photographic experience. Isopel Berners is herself a creation ranking among the fine creations of womanhood of the finest writers. I doubt not but that it was inspired by some actual memory of Borrow—the memory of some early love affair in which the distractions of his mania for word-learning—the Armenian and other languages—led him to pass by some opportunity of his life, losing the substance for the shadow. But whether there were ever a real Isopel we shall never know. We do know that Borrow has presented his fictitious one with infinite poetry and fine imaginative power. We do know, moreover, that it is not right to describe Isopel Berners as a marvellous episode in a narrative of other texture. *Lavengro* is full of marvellous episodes. Some one has ventured to comment upon Borrow's style—to imply that it is not always on a high plane. What does that matter? Style is not the quality that makes a book live, but the novelty of the ideas. Stevenson was a splendid stylist, and his admirers have deluded themselves into believing that he was, therefore, among the immortals. But Stevenson had nothing new to tell the world, and he was not, he is not, therefore of the immortals. Borrow is of the immortals, not by virtue of a style, but by virtue of having something new to say. He is with Dickens and with Carlyle as one of the three great British prose writers of the age we call Victorian, who in quite different ways have presented a new note for their own time and for long after. It is the distinction of Borrow that he has invested the common life of the road, of the highway, the path through the meadow, the gypsy encampment, the country fair, the very apple stall and wayside inn with an air of romance that can never leave those of us who have once come under the magnificent spell of *Lavengro* and the *Romany Rye*. Perhaps Borrow is pre-eminently the writer for those who sit in armchairs and dream of adventures they will never undertake. Perhaps he will never be the favourite author of the really adventurous spirit, who wants the real thing, the latest book of actual travel. But to be the favourite author of those who sit in arm-chairs is no small thing, and, as I have said already, Borrow stands with Carlyle and Dickens in *our* century, by which I mean the nineteenth century; with Defoe and Goldsmith in the eighteenth century, as one of the really great and imperishable masters of our tongue.

What then will Norwich do for George Borrow? I ask this question, although it would, perhaps, be an impertinence to ask it were I not a Norwich man. If you have read Dr. Knapp's *Life of Borrow*, you will have seen more than one reference to Mrs. Borrow's landlord, "old King," "Tom King the carpenter," and so on, who owned the house in Willow Lane in which Borrow spent his boyhood. That 'old King the carpenter'—I believe he called himself a builder, but perhaps this was when he grew more prosperous—was my great-great-uncle. One of his sons became physician to Prince Talleyrand and married a sister of John Stuart Mill. One of his great-nieces was my grandmother, and her mother's family, the Parkers, had lived in Norwich for many generations. So on the strength of this little piece of genealogy let me claim, not only to be a good Borrovian, but also a good Norvicensian. Grant me then a right to plead for a practical recognition of Borrow in the city that he loved most, although he sometimes scolded it as it often scolded him. I should like to see a statue, or some similar memorial. If you pass through the cities of the Continent—French, German, or Belgian—you will find in well-nigh every town a memorial to this or that worthy connected with its literary or artistic fame. How many memorials has Norwich to the people connected with its literary or artistic fame? Nay, I am not rash and impetuous. I would beg any one of my hearers who thinks that Borrow might well have a memorial in marble or bronze in your city to wait a while. You are busy with a statue to Sir Thomas Browne—a most commendable scheme. To attempt to raise one to Borrow at this moment would probably be to court disaster. Nor do I advocate a memorial by private subscription. Observation has shown me what that means: failure or half failure in nearly every case. The memorial when it comes must be initiated by the City Fathers in council assembled. That time is perhaps far distant. But let us all do everything we can to make secure the high and honourable achievement of George Borrow, to kindle an interest in him and his writings, to extend a taste for the undoubted beauties of his works among all classes of his fellow-citizens—that is to secure Borrow the best of all monuments. More durable than brass will be the memorial that is contained in the assurance that he possesses the reverence and the homage of all true Norfolk hearts.

IV

TO THE IMMORTAL MEMORY OF
GEORGE CRABBE

An Address delivered at the Crabbe Celebration at Aldeburgh in Suffolk on the 16th of September, 1905.

I have been asked to say something in praise of George Crabbe. The task would be an easier one were it not for the presence of the distinguished critic from the University of Nancy who is with us to-day. M. Huchon {97} has devoted to the subject a singleminded zeal to which one whose profession is primarily that of a journalist can make no claim. Moreover it has been well said that *the judgment of foreigners is the judgment of posterity*, and I fully believe that where a writer has secured the suffrages of men of another nation than his own, he has done more for his ultimate fame than the passing and fickle favour of his countrymen can secure for him. In any case Crabbe has been praised more eloquently than almost any other modern, and this in spite of the fact that he was not read by the generation succeeding his death, nor is he read much in our own time.

If you want to read Crabbe to-day in his entirety, you must become possessed of a huge and clumsy volume of sombre appearance, small type and repellant double columns. For

Clement Shorter

fully seventy years it has not paid a publisher to reprint Crabbe's poems properly. {98} When this was achieved in 1834, the edition in eight volumes was comparatively a failure, and the promised two volumes of essays and sermons were not forthcoming in consequence. Selections from Crabbe have been many, but when all is said he has been the least read for the past sixty or seventy years of all the authors who have claims to be considered classics. The least read but perhaps the best praised—that is one point of certainty. The praise began with the politicians—with the two greatest political leaders of their age. The eloquent and noble Edmund Burke, the great- hearted Charles James Fox. Burke "made" George Crabbe as no poet was ever made before or since. To me there is no picture in all literature more unflaggingly interesting than that of the great man, whose life was so full of affairs, taking the poor young stranger by the hand, reading through his abundant manuscripts, and therefrom selecting—as the poet was quite unable to select— *The Library* and *The Village* as the most suitable for publication, helping him to a publisher, introducing him to friends, and proving himself quite untiring on his behalf. There is a letter of Burke's printed in a little known book— *The Correspondence of Sir Thomas Hanmer*, Speaker of the House of Commons—in which Burke takes the trouble to defend Crabbe's moral character and to press his claims for being admitted to holy orders. "Dudley North tells me," he continues, "that he has the best character possible among those with whom he has always lived, that he is now working hard to qualify, and has not only Latin, but some smattering of Greek." It had its gracious amenities, that eighteenth century, for I do not believe that there is a man in the ranks of the present Government, or of the present Opposition, who would take all this trouble for a poor unknown who had appealed to him merely by two or three long letters recounting his career. Nay, Cabinet Ministers are less punctilious than formerly, and the newest type, I understand, leaves letters unanswered. I can imagine the attitude of one of our modern statesmen in the face of two quite bulky packages of many sheets from a young author. He would request his secretary to see what they were all about, and then would follow the curt answer—"I am directed by Dash to say that he cannot comply with your request." Burke not only wrote to the Speaker of the House of Commons, but enclosed Crabbe's letter to him, a quite wonderful piece of autobiography. {100} All Crabbe's admirers should read that letter. Crabbe apologizes for writing again, and refers to "these repeated attacks on your patience." "My father," he said, "had a place in the Custom House at Aldeburgh. He had a large family, a little income and no economy," and then the story of his life up to that time is told to Burke in fullest detail.

Again, there is that other statesman-admirer of Crabbe, Charles James Fox. Fox gave to Crabbe's work an admiration which never faltered, and on his death-bed requested that the pathetic story of Phoebe Dawson in *The Parish Register* should be read to him—it was, we are told, "the last piece of poetry that soothed his dying ear."

In Lord Holland's *Memoirs of the Whig Party* there is a statement by his nephew which no biographer so far has quoted:—

> I read over to him the whole of Crabbe's *Parish Register* in manuscript. Some parts he made me read twice; he remarked several passages as exquisitely beautiful, and objected to some few which I mentioned to the author and which he, in almost every instance, altered before publication. Mr. Fox repeated once or twice that it was a very pretty poem, that Crabbe's condition in the world had improved since he wrote *The Village*, and his view of life, likewise *The Parish Register*, bore marks of considerably

more indulgence to our species; though not so many as he could have wished, especially as the few touches of that nature were beautiful in the extreme. He was particularly struck with the description of the substantial happiness of a farmer's wife.

From great novelists the tributes are not less noteworthy than from great statesmen. Jane Austen, whose personality perhaps has more real womanly attractiveness than that of any sister novelist of the first rank, declared playfully that if she could have been persuaded to change her state it would have been to become Mrs. Crabbe; and who can forget Sir Walter Scott's request in his last illness: "Read me some amusing thing—read me a bit of Crabbe." They read to him from *The Borough*, and we all remember his comment, "Capital—excellent—very good." Yet at this time—in 1832—any popularity that Crabbe had once enjoyed was already on the wane. Other idols had caught the popular taste, and from that day to this there was to be no real revival of appreciation for these poems. There were to be no lack of admirers, however, of the audience "fit though few." Byron's praise has been too often quoted for repetition. Wordsworth, who rarely praised his contemporaries in poetry, declared of Crabbe that his works "would last from their combined merit as poetry and truth." Macaulay writes of "that incomparable passage in Crabbe's *Borough* which has made many a rough and cynical reader cry like a child"—the passage in which the condemned felon

Takes his tasteless food, and when 'tis done,
Counts up his meals, now lessen'd by that one,—

a story which Macaulay bluntly charges Robert Montgomery with stealing. Lord Tennyson, again, at a much later date, admitted that "Crabbe has a world of his own."

Not less impressive surely is the attitude of the two writers as far as the poles asunder in their outlook upon life and its mysteries—Cardinal Newman and Edward FitzGerald. The famous theologian, we learn from the *Letters and Correspondence* collected by Anne Mozley, writes in 1820 of his "excessive fondness" for *The Tales of the Hall*, and thirty years later in one of his *Discourses* he says of Crabbe's poems that they are among "the most touching in our language." Still another twenty years, and the aged cardinal reread Crabbe to find that he was more delighted than ever with our poet. That great nineteenth century pagan, on the other hand, that prince of letter-writers and wonderful poet of whom Suffolk has also reason to be proud, Edward FitzGerald, was even more ardent. Praise of Crabbe is scattered freely throughout the many volumes of his correspondence, and he edited, as we all know, a book of Selections, which I want to see reprinted. It contains a preface that, it may be admitted, is not really worthy of FitzGerald, so lacking is it in the force and vigour of his correspondence. But this also was in fact yet another death-bed tribute, for it was, I think, one of the last things FitzGerald wrote. FitzGerald, however, has done more for Crabbe among the moderns than any other man. His keen literary judgment must have brought new converts to that limited brotherhood of the elect, of which this gathering forms no inconsiderable portion.

We have one advantage in speaking about George Crabbe that does not obtain with any other poet of great eminence; that is to say, that his life story has not been hackneyed by repetition. With almost any other writer there is some standing biography which is widely familiar. The *Life of George Crabbe*, written by his son, although it is one of the very best biographies that I have ever read, is little known. It was quite out of print for years, and it has never been reprinted separately from the poems. It is an admirable biography, and it offers a contradiction of the view occasionally urged that a man's life should not be written by a member of his own family; for George Crabbe the second would seem not only to have been an exceedingly able man, but possessed of a frankness of disposition in criticizing his father which sons are often prone to show in real life, but which, I imagine, they rarely show in print. His book is a model of candid statement, treating of Crabbe's little weaknesses—and who of us has not his little weaknesses—in the most cheery possible manner. It is perhaps a small matter to tell us in one place of his father's want of "taste," his insensibility to the beauty of order in his composition—that had been done by the critics before him; but he even has something to say about the philandering which characterized the old gentleman in the last years of his life, his apparent anxiety to get married again. {106} The only thing that he all but ignores is Crabbe's opium habit—a habit that came to him as a sedative from a painful complaint and inspired, as was the case with Coleridge, his more melodious utterances. Taken altogether the picture is as pleasant as it is capable and exhaustive. We see his early boyhood at Aldeburgh, his schooldays: his first period of unhappiness at Slaughden Quay, his apprenticeship near Bury St. Edmunds, where we seem to hear his master's daughters, when he reached the door, exclaim with laughter, "La! Here's our new 'prentice." We follow him a little higher, to the house of the Woodbridge surgeon, then through his prolonged courtship of Sarah Elmy, then to those dreary, uncongenial duties of piling up butter casks on Slaughden Quay. A brief period of starvation in London, and we find him again in a chemist's shop in Aldeburgh. Lastly comes his most important journey to London upon the borrowed sum of 5 pounds, only three of which he carried in hard cash. His hand to mouth existence in London for some months is among the most interesting things in literature. Chatterton's tragic fate might have been his, but, more fortunate than Chatterton, he had friends at

Beccles who helped him, and he was even able to publish a poem, *The Candidate*. Although this poem contained only thirty-four pages, one is not quite sure but that it helped to ruin its publisher. In any case that publisher went bankrupt soon after.

Crabbe has been reproached for having continually attempted to secure a "patron" at this time, and it has been hinted by Sir Leslie Stephen that he ought to have recognized that the patron was out of date, killed by Dr. Johnson's sturdy defiance. I do not agree with this view. Dr. Johnson, in spite of his famous epigram, was always more or less assisted by the patron, although his personality was strong enough to enable him to turn the tables at the end. When one comes to think of it, Thrale the brewer was a patron of Johnson, so was Strahan the printer. And does he not say in his famous letter to Lord Chesterfield that "Seven years, my lord, have now passed since I waited in your outward rooms, or was repulsed from your door," clearly implying that if Chesterfield was not Johnson's patron it was not the great Doctor's fault? In any case the patron must always exist for the poor man of letters in every age. Now, he is frequently a collective personality rather than an individual. He is represented for the author who has tried and failed by the Royal Literary Fund, by such bounty as is awarded by the Society of Authors, or by the Civil List Grant. For the author in embryo he is assisted above all by the literary log-roller who flourishes so much in our day. If he is not this "collective personality," or one of the others I have named, then he is something much worse—that is, a capitalist publisher. We can none of us who have to earn a living run away from the patronage of capital, and when Sir Leslie Stephen was being paid a salary by the late Mr. George Smith for editing the *Dictionary of National Biography*, and was told, as we remember that he frequently was, that it was not a remunerative venture and that, as Mr.

Smith was fond of saying, his publishing business did not pay for his vineries, Sir Leslie Stephen was experiencing a patronage, if he had known it, not less melancholy than anything Crabbe suffered from Edmund Burke or the Duke of Rutland.

When one meets a writer who desires to walk on high stilts and to talk of the independence of literature, one is entitled to ask him if it was a greater indignity for Lord Tennyson in his younger days to have received 200 pounds a year from the Civil List than for Crabbe to have received the same sum as the Duke of Rutland's chaplain; in fact, Crabbe earned the money, and Tennyson did not. There are, as I have said, some most wonderful and pathetic touches in the account of Crabbe's attempt to conquer London. There are his letters to his sweetheart, for example, his "dearest Mira," in one of which he says that he is possessed of 6.25*d.* in the world. In another he relates that he has sold his surgical instruments in order to pay his bills. Nevertheless, we find him standing at a bookstall where he sees Dryden's works in three volumes, octavo, for five shillings, and of his few shillings he ventures to offer 3*s.* 6*d.*—and carries home the Dryden. What bibliophile but must love such a story as that, even though a day or two afterwards its hero writes, "My last shilling became 8*d.* yesterday." But what a good investment withal. Dryden made him a much better poet. Then comes the famous letter to Burke, and the less known second letter to which I have referred, and Burke's splendid reception of the writer. Nothing, I repeat, in the life of any great man is more beautiful than that. As Crabbe's son finely says: "He went in Burke's room a poor young adventurer, spurned by the opulent and rejected by the publishers, his last shilling gone, and his last hope with it. He came out virtually secure of almost all the good fortune that by successive stages afterwards fell to his lot." The success that comes to most men is built up on such chances, on the kind help of some one or other individual.

Finally there came—for I am hastily recapitulating Crabbe's story—the years of prosperity, curacies, rectories, the praise of great contemporaries, but nothing surely more edifying than the burning of piles of manuscripts so extensive that no fireplace would hold them. The son's account of his assisting at these conflagrations is not the least interesting part of his biography, the merits of which I desire to emphasize.

People who make jokes about that most succulent edible, the crab, when the poet Crabbe is mentioned in their presence— and who can resist an obvious pun—are not really far astray. There can be little doubt but that a remote ancestor of George Crabbe took his name from the "shellfish," as we all persist, in spite of the naturalist, in calling it; and the poet did not hesitate to attribute it to the vanity of an ancestor that his name had had two letters added. Nor when we hear of Cromer crabs, or crabs from some other part of Norfolk as distinct from what I am sure is equally palatable, the crustacean as it may be found in Aldeburgh, are we remote from the story of our poet's life. For there cannot be a doubt but that Norfolk shares with Suffolk the glory of his origin. His family, it is clear, came first from Norfolk. The Crabbes of Norfolk were farmers, the Crabbes of Suffolk always favoured the seacoast, and all the glory that surrounds the name of the poet to whom we do honour to-day is reflected in the town in which he was born and bred. Aldeburgh is Crabbe's own town, and it is an interesting fact that no other poet can be identified with one particular spot in the way in which Crabbe can be identified with this beautiful watering-place in which we are now assembled. Shakspere was more of a Londoner than a Stratfordian; nearly all his best work was written in London, and many of the most receptive years of his life were spent in that city. Milton's honoured name is identified with many places, apart from London, the city of his birth. Shelley, Byron and Keats were essentially cosmopolitans in their writings as in their lives. Wordsworth was closely identified with Grasmere, although born in a neighbouring county; but he went to many and varied scenes, and to more than one country, for some of his most inspired verses. Then Cowper, the poet of whom one most often thinks when one is recalling the achievement of Crabbe, is a poet of some half- dozen places other than Olney, and perhaps his best verses were written at Weston-Underwood. Now George Crabbe in the years of his success was identified with many places other than Aldeburgh: with Belvoir Castle, with Muston, and with Trowbridge, where he died, and some of his admirers have even identified him with Bath. When all this is allowed, it is upon Aldeburgh that the whole of his writings turned, the place where he was born, where he spent his boyhood, and the earlier years of a perhaps too sordid manhood, whither he returned twice, as a chemist's assistant and as curate. It is the place that primarily inspired all his verses. Aldeburgh stands out vividly before us in each succeeding poem—in *The Village*, *The Borough*, *The Parish Register*, *The Tales*, and even in those *Tales of the Hall*, composed in later life in faraway Trowbridge. Crabbe's vivid observations indeed come home to every one who has studied his works when they have visited not only Aldeburgh but its vicinity. Every reach of the river Ald recalls some striking line by him: the scenery in *The Lover's Journey* we know is a description of the road between Aldeburgh and Beccles, and all who have sailed along the river to Orford have recognized that no stream has been so perfectly portrayed by a poet's pen. Here in his writings you may have a suggestion of Muston, here of Allington, and here again of Trowbridge; but in the main it is the Suffolk scenery that most of us here know so well that was ever in his mind.

When an attempt was once made to stir up the Great Eastern

Railway to identify this district with the name of Crabbe as the English Lakes were identified with the name of Wordsworth, and the Scots Lakes with that of Sir Walter Scott, a high official of the railway made the statement that up to that moment he had never even heard the name of Crabbe. Well, all that is going to be changed. I do not at all approve of the phrase beloved of certain book-makers and of railway companies that implies that any county or district is the monopoly of one man, be he ever so great a writer. Yet I venture to say that within the next ten years the "Crabbe Country" will sound as familiar to the officials of the Great Eastern as the "Wordsworth Country" does to those of the Midland or the North Western. It is true that once in the bitterness of his heart the poet referred to Aldeburgh as "a little venal borough in Suffolk" and that he more than once alluded to his unkind reception upon his reappearance as a curate, when he had previously failed at other callings. "In my own village they think nothing of me," he once said. But who does not know how the heart turns with the years to the places associated with childhood and youth, and Crabbe was a remarkable exemplification of this. A well-known literary journal stated only last week that "Crabbe's connexion with Aldeburgh was not very protracted." So far from this being true it would be no exaggeration to say that it extended over the whole of his seventy-eight years of life. It included the first five-and-twenty years almost entirely. It included also the brief curacy, the prolonged residence at Parham and Glenham, frequent visits for holidays in after years, and who but a lover of his native place would have done as his son pictures him doing when at Stathern—riding alone to the coast of Lincolnshire, sixty miles from where he was living, only to dip in the waves that also washed the beach of Aldeburgh and returned immediately to his home. "There is no sea like the Aldeburgh sea," said Edward FitzGerald, and we may be sure that was Crabbe's opinion also, for revisiting it in later life he wrote:—

There once again, my native place I come
Thee to salute, my earliest, latest home.

One picture in Crabbe's life stands out vividly to us all—the long years of devotion given by him to Sarah Elmy, and the reciprocal devotion of the very capable woman who finally became his wife. Crabbe's courtship and marriage affords a pleasant contrast to the usual unhappy relations of poets with their wives. Shakspere, Milton, Dryden, Byron, Shelley, and many another poet was less happy in this respect, and I am not sure how far the belief in Crabbe's powers as a poet has been affected by the fact that he lived on the whole a happy, humdrum married life. The public has so long been accustomed to expect a different state of things.

I have given thus much time to Crabbe's life story because it interests me, and I do not believe that it is possible nowadays to kindle a very profound interest in any writer without a definite presentation of his personality. Apart from his biography—his three biographies by George Crabbe the second, Mr. T. E. Kebbel, and Canon Ainger, there are the seven volumes of his works. Now I do not imagine that any great accession will be made to the ranks of Crabbe's admirers by asking people to take down these seven volumes and read them right through—a thing I have myself done twice, and many here also I doubt not. Rather would I plead for a reprint of Edmund FitzGerald's Selections, or failing that I would ask you to look at the volume of Selections made by Mr. Bernard Holland, or that other admirable selection by the Rev. Anthony Deane. "I must think my old Crabbe will come up again, though never to be popular," wrote FitzGerald to Archbishop Trench. Well, perhaps the "large still books" of the older writers are never destined to be popular again, but they will always maintain with genuine book lovers their place in English Literature, and if the adequate praise they have received from many good judges is well kept to the front there will be constant accessions to the ranks, and readers will want the whole of Crabbe's works in which to dig for themselves. Crabbe's place in English Literature needed not such a gathering as this to make it secure, but we want celebrations of our literary heroes to keep alive enthusiasm, and to encourage the faint-hearted.

In the glorious tradition of English Literature, then, Crabbe comes after Cowper and before Wordsworth. There is a lineal descent as clear and well-defined as any set forth in the peerages of "Burke" or "Debrett." We read in vain if we do not fully grasp the continuity of creative work. Cowper was born in 1731, Crabbe in 1754, and Cowper was called to the Bar in the year that Crabbe was born. In spite of this disparity of years they started upon their literary careers almost at the same time. *The Village* was published in 1783, and *The Task* in 1785, yet Cowper is in every sense the elder poet, inheriting more closely the traditions of Pope and Dryden, coming less near to humanity than Crabbe, and being more emphatically a child of the eighteenth century in its artificial aspects. It is impossible to indict a whole century with all its varied accomplishments, and the century that produced Swift and Cowper and Crabbe had no lack of the finer instincts of brotherhood. Yet the century was essentially a cruel one. Take as an example the attitude of naturally kindly men to the hanging of Dr. Dodd for forgery. Even Samuel Johnson, who did what he could for Dodd, did not find, as he should have done, his whole soul revolted by such a punishment for a crime against property. Cowper has immense claim upon our regard. He is one of the truest of poets, and one of the most interesting figures in all English literature, although no small share of his one-time popularity was due to his identification with Evangelicalism in religion. Cowper had humour and other qualities which enabled him to make the universal appeal to all hearts which is the test of the greatest literature—the appeal of "John Gilpin," the

"Lines" to his Mother's Portrait, and his verses on "The loss of the *Royal George*." Crabbe made no such appeal, and he has not the adventitious assistance that association with a religious sect affords. Hence the popularity he once enjoyed was more entirely on his merits than was that of Cowper. He was the first of the eighteenth century poets who was able to *see things as they really are*. Therein lies his strength. Were they poets at all—those earlier eighteenth century writers? It sounds like rank blasphemy to question it, but what is poetry? Surely it is the expression artistically in rhythmic form—or even without it—of the sincerest emotions concerning nature and life. The greatest poet is not the one who is most sincere—a very bad poet can be that—but the poet who expresses that sincerity with the most perfect art. From this point of view the poets before Cowper and Crabbe, Pope, Goldsmith, Johnson and others were scarcely poets at all. Masters of language every one of them, able to command a fine rhetoric, but not poets. Gray in two or three pieces was a poet, but for Johnson that claim can scarcely be made. Cowper was the first to emancipate himself from the conventionality of his age, and Crabbe emancipated himself still further. He had boundless sincerity, and he is really a very great poet even if he has not the perfection of art of some later poets. Many know Crabbe only by the parody of his manner in *Rejected Addresses*:

John Richard William Alexander Dwyer
Was footman to Justinian Stubbs Esquire;
But when John Dwyer listed in the blues,
Emanuel Jennings polished Stubbs's shoes.

and it must be admitted that there are plenty of lines like these in Crabbe, as for example:—

Grave Jonas Kindred, Sybil Kindred's sire
Was six feet high, and looked six inches higher.

or this:—

> The church he view'd as liberal minds will view
> And there he fixed his principles and pew.

Banalities of this kind are scattered through his pages as they are scattered through those of Wordsworth. Nevertheless he was a great poet, bringing us before Wordsworth out of the ruck of artificiality and insincerity. Does any one suppose that Pope in his *Essay on Man*, that Johnson in his *London* or that Goldsmith in his *Deserted Village* had any idea other than the production of splendid phrases. Each and all of them were brilliant men of letters. Crabbe was not a brilliant man of letters, but he was a fine and a genuine poet. You will look in vain in his truest work for the lyrical and musical gift that we associate with poets who came after:—Shelley, Keats, Tennyson—poets who made Crabbe's work quite distasteful for some three generations. Crabbe it has been claimed had that gift also, to be found in "Sir Eustace Grey" and other verses written under the inspiration of opium, as much of Coleridge's best work was written—but it is not in these that his admirers will seek to emphasize his achievement—it is in his work which treats of

> The simple annals of my parish poor.

The Village, The Parish Register, The Borough, and many of the *Tales* bear witness to a clear vision of life as it is lived by the majority of people born into this world. I have seen criticism of Crabbe which calls him the poet who took the middle classes for his subjects, criticism which compared him with George Eliot. All this is quite beside the mark. Crabbe is pre-eminently the poet of the poor, with a lesson for to-day as much as for a century ago. Villages are not now what they were then, we are told. But I fully believe that there are all the conditions of life to-day hidden beneath the

Clement Shorter

surface as Crabbe's close observations pictured them. "The altered position of the poor," says Mr. Courthope, "has fortunately deprived his poems of much of the reality they once possessed." I do not believe it. The closely packed towns, the herding together of families, the squalor are still to be found in our midst. Crabbe has his message for our time as well as for his own. How he tore the veil from the conventional language of his day, the picture of the ideal village where the happy peasantry passed through life so joyously. Contrast such pictures with his sad declaration—

I've seldom known, though I have often read
Of happy peasants on their dying-bed.

Solution Crabbe offers none for the tragedy of poverty. He was no politician. He signed the nomination paper for John Wilson Croker the Tory in his native Aldeburgh, and he supported a Whig at the same election at Trowbridge. His politics were summed up in backing his friends of both parties. But he did see, as politicians are only beginning to see to-day, that the ultimate solution was a social one and not a mere question of political parties. Generations have passed away since he lived, and men are still shouting themselves hoarse to prove that in this Shibboleth or in that may be found the salvation of the country, yet we have still our thousands on the verge of starvation, we have still the very poor in our midst, and the problem seems as far from solution as ever. But it would be all the better for the State if we could keep the questions raised by Crabbe in his wonderful pictures more continually in view,—lacking in taste as they may sometimes seem to weak stomachs, coarse, unvarnished narratives though they be of a life which is really almost entirely sordid.

Then let us turn to Crabbe's gallery of pictures. Phoebe Dawson, and the equally pathetic Ruth, Blaney and Clelia,

Peter Grimes and many another. They are as clearly defined a set of entirely human beings as any Master has given us. It is not assuredly in George Eliot, as Canon Ainger suggests, that I find an affinity to Crabbe among the moderns, but in two much greater writers of quite different texture, Balzac and Dickens. Had Crabbe not been bounded and restrained by the conventions of his cloth, he might have become one of the most popular story-tellers in our literature—the English Balzac. At a hundred points Charles Dickens is an entire contrast to Crabbe—in his buoyant humour, his gaiety of heart, in the glamour that he throws over the life of the poor, a glamour that was more present in the early Victorian era than in our own, but Crabbe is with Balzac and with Dickens in that he presents as no other moderns have done living pictures of suffering human lives.

There is yet one other literary force, powerful in our day, that has been largely influenced by Crabbe. Those who love the novels of Mr. Thomas Hardy, whom we rejoice to see with us at this Celebration,—his *Woodlanders*, *The Return of the Native*, *Far from the Madding Crowd*, and many another book that touches the very heart of things in nature and human life, will rejoice to hear that this great writer has admitted George Crabbe to be the most potent influence that has affected his work. I have heard him declare many times how much he was inspired by Crabbe, whereas the later French realists had no influence upon him whatever. "Crabbe was our first great English realist" Mr. Hardy would tell you if only we could persuade him to speak from this platform, as unfortunately he will not.

Lastly let us take Crabbe as a great story-teller. He has many more ideas than most of the novelists. That is why we do well to recall the hint of the writer who said that when a new work came out we should take down an old one from our shelves. Instead of the "un-idead" novels, that come out by the dozen and are so popular. I wish we could agree to read Crabbe's novels in verse. Unhappily their form is against them in the present age. But it would not be at all a misfortune if we could make Crabbe's *Tales* once more the vogue. They are good stories, absorbingly interesting. They leave a very vivid impression on the mind. Once read they are unforgettable.

I have seen it stated that these stories are old-fashioned both in manner and in substance. In manner they may be, but in substance I maintain they are intensely modern, alive with the spirit of our time. Any latter- day novelist might envy Crabbe his power of developing a story. It is this essential modernity that is to make Crabbe's place in English literature secure for generations yet to come.

Finally, Crabbe's place in English literature is as the bridge between the eighteenth and nineteenth century. With him begins that "enthusiasm of humanity" which the eighteenth century so imperfectly understood. Byron and Wordsworth, disliking each other cordially, did well to praise him, for he was their forerunner. A master of pathos, you may find in his work incentive to tears and laughter, although sometimes the humour, as in *The Learned Boy*, is sadly unconscious.

But I must bring these rambling remarks to a close, and in doing so I must once again quote that other Suffolk worthy to whom many of us are very much attached, I mean Edward FitzGerald. When Sir Leslie Stephen wrote what is to my mind a singularly infelicitous essay on Crabbe in the *Cornhill*, he quoted the remark, which seemed to be new to FitzGerald, as to Crabbe being a "pope in worsted stockings"—a remark made by Horace Smith of *Rejected Addresses*, although I have seen it ascribed to Byron and others. "Pope in worsted stockings," exclaimed FitzGerald, "why I could cite whole paragraphs of as fine a texture as

Moliere; 'incapable of epigram,' the jackanapes says—why, I could find fifty of the very best epigrams in five minutes," and later, in another letter he writes—

I am positively looking over my everlasting Crabbe again; he naturally comes in about the fall of the year.

Here surely is an appropriate quotation, a little prophetic perhaps, for our gathering—the "everlasting Crabbe." We cannot all love Crabbe as much as FitzGerald loved him, but this gathering will not be vain if after this we handle his volumes more lovingly, read his poems more sympathetically, and continue with more zeal than ever before to be proud of the man who, born in Aldeburgh a century and a half ago, is closely identified with this county of Suffolk as I believe no other great writer is closely identified with any county in England. An Aldeburgh man—a Suffolk man he was—yet even more in the future than in the past, he is destined to gain the whole world for his parish. He is the everlasting Crabbe!

V

THE LITERARY ASSOCIATIONS OF EAST ANGLIA

An address to the East Anglian Society on the occasion of a
dinner to Mr. William Dutt, author of "Highways and
Byways in East Anglia." March 25, 1901.

I appreciate the privilege of being allowed to speak this
evening for a few minutes upon the literary associations of
East Anglia, of being permitted to ask you, while doing
honour to a well-known East Anglian writer of to-day, to
cast a glance back upon the literature of the past so far as it
affects that portion of the British Empire with which we
nearly all of us here are proud to be associated. There is
necessarily some difference of opinion as to what constitutes
East Anglia. I find that our guest of to-night tells us that it is
"Norfolk, Suffolk and portions of Essex, Cambridgeshire and
Lincolnshire." Dr. Knapp, the biographer of Borrow, says
that it is Norfolk, Suffolk and Cambridgeshire; personally I
am content with that classification, because, although I was
born in London, I claim, apart from schoolboy days at
Downham Market, a pretty lengthy ancestry from Norwich
on one side—which is indisputably East Anglia—and from
Welney, near Wisbeach, on another side, and Welney and
Wisbeach are, I affirm, just as much East Anglia as Norwich
and Ipswich. With reference to those other counties and

portions of counties, I think that the inhabitants must be allowed to decide for themselves. I imagine that they will give every possible stretch to the imagination in order to allow themselves the honour of being incorporated in East Anglia, a name that one never pronounces without recalling that fine old-world compliment of St. Augustine of Canterbury to our ancestors, that they ought to be called not "Angles" but "Angels."

Every one in particular who loves books must be proud to partake of our great literary tradition. If it is difficult to decide precisely what East Anglia is, it is perhaps equally difficult to speak for a few minutes on so colossal a theme as the literature of East Anglia. It would be easy to recapitulate what every biographical dictionary will provide, a long list of famous names associated with our counties; to remind you that we have produced two poet-laureates—John Skelton, of Diss, the author of *Colyn Cloute*, and Thomas Shadwell, of Broomhill, the playwright—the latter perhaps not entirely a subject for pride; two very rough and ready political philosophers, Thomas Paine, born at Thetford, and William Godwin, born at Wisbeach; a very popular novelist in Bulwer Lytton, and a very popular theologian in Dr. Samuel Clarke; as also the famous brother and sister whose works appealed to totally different minds, James and Harriet Martineau. Then there was that pathetic creature and indifferent poet, Robert Bloomfield, whose *Farmer's Boy* once appeared in the luxurious glories of an expensive quarto. Finally, one recalls that two of the most popular women writers of an earlier generation, Clara Reeve, the novelist, and Agnes Strickland, the historian, were Suffolk women.

But I am not concerned to give you a recapitulation of all the East Anglian writers, whose names, as I have said, can be found in any biographical dictionary, and the quality of whose work would rather suggest that East Anglia, from a

Clement Shorter

literary point of view, is a land of extinct volcanoes. I am naturally rather anxious to make use of the golden opportunity that has been afforded me to emphasize my own literary sympathies, and to say in what I think lies the glory of East Anglia, at least so far as the creation of books is concerned. Here I make an interesting claim for East Anglia, that it has given us in Captain Marryat perhaps the very greatest prose writer of the nineteenth century who has been a delight to youth, and two of the very greatest prose writers of all times for the inspiration of middle-age, Sir Thomas Browne and George Borrow. It has given us in Sarah Austin an example of a learned woman who was also a fascinating woman; it has given us again the most remarkable letter-writers in the English language—Margaret Paston, Horace Walpole and Edward FitzGerald. To these there were only three serious rivals as letter-writers—William Cowper, Thomas Grey and Charles Lamb; and the first found a final home and a last resting-place in our midst. It has given us that remarkable novelist and entertaining diarist, Fanny Burney. Finally, it has given us in that same William Cowper—who rests in East Dereham Church, and for whom we claim on that and for other reasons some share and participation in his genius—a great and much loved poet. It has given us indeed in William Cowper and George Crabbe the two most natural and the two most human poets in the English literature of two centuries, only excepting the favourite poet of Scotland—Robert Burns. It is to these of all writers that I would pin my faith in talking of East Anglia and its literature; it is their names that I would have you keep in your mind when you call up memories of the literature which has most inspired our East Anglian life.

In connexion with many writers a point of importance will occur to us. Only occasionally has a great English author a special claim on one particular portion of England. He has not been the lesser or the greater for that, it has merely been an accident of his birth and of his career. The greatest of all writers, the one of whom all Englishmen are naturally the most proud, Shakspere, has, it is true, an abundant association with Warwickshire, but Shakspere stands almost alone in this, as in many things. Chaucer, Spenser, Milton, Byron and Keats were born in London; they travelled widely, they lived in many different counties or countries, and cannot be said to have adorned any distinctively local tradition. Shelley was born in Sussex, but a hundred cities, including Rome, where his ashes rest, may claim some participation in his fine spirit. Wordsworth, on the other hand, who was born in Cumberland, certainly obtained the greater part of his inspiration from the neighbouring county of Westmorland, where his life was passed. But when we come to East Anglia we are face to face with a body of writers who belong to the very soil, upon whom the particular character of the landscape has had a permanent effect, who are not only very great Englishmen and Englishwomen, but are great East Anglians as well.

I have said that Captain Marryat was an East Anglian, and have we not a right to be proud of Marryat's breezy stories of the sea? Our youth has found such plentiful stimulus in *Peter Simple*, *Frank Mildmay*, and *Mr. Midshipman Easy*; generations of boys have read them with delight, generations of boys will read them. And not only boys, but men. One recalls that Carlyle, in one of his deepest fits of depression, took refuge in Marryat's novels with infinite advantage to his peace of mind. Speaking of Captain Marryat and books for boys, a quite minor kind of literature perhaps some of you may think, I must recall that an earlier and still more famous story for children had an East Anglian origin. Did not The Babes in the Wood come out of Norfolk? Was it not their estate in that county that, as we learn from Percy's *Reliques*, their wicked uncle coveted, and were not the last hours of those unfortunate children, in this most picturesque and

　　　　　Clement Shorter

pathetic of stories, solaced by East Anglian robins and their poor bodies covered by East Anglian vegetation?

Let me pass, however, to what may be counted more serious literature. What can one say of Sir Thomas Browne unless indeed one has an hour in which to say it. Every page of that great writer's *Religio Medici* and *Urn Burial* is quotable—full of worldly wisdom and of an inspiration that is not of the world. Browne was born in London, and not until he was thirty-two years of age did he settle in Norwich, where he was "much resorted to for his skill in physic," and where he lived for forty-five years, when the fine church of St. Peter Mancroft, received his ashes—a church in which, let me add, with pardonable pride, my own grandfather and grandmother were married. I am glad that Norwich is shortly to commemorate by a fitting monument not the least great of her sons, one who has been aptly called "the English Montaigne." {138}

Perhaps there are those who would dispute my claim for Marryat and for Sir Thomas Browne that they were East Anglians—both were only East Anglians by adoption. There are even those who dispute the claim for one whom I must count well-nigh the greatest of East Anglian men of letters—George Borrow. Borrow, I maintain, was an East Anglian if ever there was one, although this has been questioned by Mr. Theodore Watts- Dunton. Now I have the greatest possible regard for Mr. Watts-Dunton. He is distinguished alike as a critic, a poet, and a romancer. But I must join issue with him here, and you, I know, will forgive me for taking up your time with the matter; for if Mr. Watts-Dunton were right, one of the chief glories would be shorn from our East Anglian traditions. He denies in the Introduction to a new edition of *The Romany Rye*, just published, the claim of Borrow to be an East Anglian, although Borrow himself insisted that he was one.

One might as well call Charlotte Bronte a Yorkshire woman as call Borrow an East Anglian. He was no more an East Anglian than an Irishman born in London is an Englishman. His father was a Cornishman and his mother of French extraction. Not one drop of East Anglian blood was in the veins of Borrow's father, and very little in the veins of his mother. Borrow's ancestry was pure Cornish on one side, and on the other mainly French. But such was the egotism of Borrow that the fact of his having been born in East Anglia made him look upon that part of the world as the very hub of the universe.

Well, I am not prepared to question the suggestion that East Anglia is the hub of the universe, only to question Mr. Watts-Dunton's position. There is virtue in that qualification of his that there was "very little" East Anglian blood in the veins of Borrow's mother, and that she was "mainly" French. As a matter of fact she was, of course, partly East Anglian; that is to say, she must have had two or three generations of East Anglian blood in her, seeing that it was her great-grandfather who settled in Norfolk from France, and he and his children and grandchildren intermarried with the race. But I do not pin my claim for Borrow upon that fact—the fact of three generations of his mother's family at Dumpling Green—or even on the fact that he was born near East Dereham. There is nothing more certain than that we are all of us influenced greatly by our environment, and that it is this, quite as much as birth or ancestry, that gives us what characteristics we possess. It is the custom, for example, to call Swift an Irishman, whereas Swift came of English parentage and lived for many of his most impressionable years in England. Nevertheless, he may be justly claimed by the sister-island, for during a long sojourn in that country he became permeated with the subtle influence of the Irish race, and in many things he thought and felt as an Irishman. It is the custom to speak of Maria Edgeworth as an Irish novelist, yet Miss Edgeworth was born in England of English parentage. Nevertheless, she was quite as much an Irish novelist as Charles Lever and Samuel Lover, for all her life was spent in direct communion with the Irish race, and her books were Irish books. It is, on the other hand, quite unreasonable to deny that Charlotte Bronte was a Yorkshire woman. Only once at the end of her life did she visit Ireland for a few weeks. Her Irish father and her Cornish mother doubtless influenced her nature in many ways, but not less certain was the influence of those wonderful moors around Haworth, and the people among whom she lived. Neither Ireland nor Cornwall has as much right to claim her as Yorkshire. I am the last to disclaim the influence of what is sometimes called "Celticism" upon English literature; upon this point I am certain that Matthew Arnold has said almost the last word. The Celts—not necessarily the Irish, as there are three or four races of Celts in addition to the Irish—have in the main given English literature its fine imaginative quality, and even where he cannot trace a Celtic origin to an English writer we may fairly assume that there is Celtic blood somewhere in an earlier generation.

Nevertheless, the impressions, as I have said, derived from environment are of the utmost vitality, and assuredly Borrow was an East Anglian, as Sir Thomas Browne was an East Anglian. In each writer you can trace the influence of our soil in a peculiar degree, and particularly in Borrow. Borrow was proud of being an East Anglian, and we are proud of him. In *Lavengro*, I venture to assert, we have the greatest example of prose style in our modern literature, and I rejoice to see a growing Borrow cult, a cult that is based not on an acceptance of the narrower side of Borrow—his furious ultra-Protestantism, for example—as was the popularity that he once enjoyed, but upon the fact that he was a magnificent artist in words. No artist in words but is influenced by environment. Charles Kingsley, for example, who came from quite different surroundings, was profoundly influenced by the East Anglian fen- country:—

> "They have a beauty of their own, those great fens," he said, "a beauty of the sea, of boundless expanse and freedom. Overhead the arch of heaven spreads more ample than elsewhere, and that vastness gives such cloud-lands, such sunrises, such sunsets, as can be seen nowhere else within these isles."

But I must hasten on, although I would fain tarry long over George Borrow and his works. I have said that East Anglia is the country of great letter writers. First, there was Margaret Paston. There is no such contribution to a remote period of English history as that contained in the *Paston Letters*, and I think we must associate them with the name of a woman— Margaret Paston. Margaret's husband, John Paston; her son, Sir John Paston; and her second son, who, strangely enough, was also a John, and called himself "John Paston the Youngest," come frequently before us in the correspondence, but Margaret Paston is the central figure.

It may not be without interest to some of my hearers who are married to recall that Margaret Paston addresses her husband not as "Dear John," or "My dear John," as I imagine a wife of to-day would do, but as "Right Reverend and Worshipful Husband." Nowhere is there such a vivid picture of a bygone age as that contained in these *Paston Letters*. We who sit quietly by the hearth in the reign of King Edward VII may read what it meant to live by the hearth in the reign of King Edward IV. It is curious that the most humane documents of far-off times in our history should all come from East Anglia, not only those *Paston Letters*, brimful of the most vital interest concerning the reigns of Henry VI and Edward IV, but also an even earlier period—the life, or at least the monastic life in the time of the first Richard and of King

Clement Shorter

John is in a most extraordinarily human fashion mirrored for us in that Chronicle of St. Edmund's Bury Monastery known as the Jocelyn Chronicle, published by the Camden Society, which Carlyle has vitalized so superbly for us in *Past and Present*.

But I was speaking of the great letter writers, commencing with Margaret Paston. Who are our greatest letter writers? Undoubtedly they are Horace Walpole, William Cowper and Edward FitzGerald. You know what a superb picture of eighteenth century life has been presented to us in the nine volumes of correspondence we have by Horace Walpole. {144} Walpole was to all practical purposes an East Anglian, although he happened to be born in London. His father, the great Sir Robert Walpole, was a notable East Anglian, and he had the closest ties of birth and association with East Anglia. Many of his letters were written from the family mansion of Houghton. {145}

Next in order comes William Cowper. I believe that more than one literary historian has claimed Cowper as a Norfolk man. Cowper was born in Hertfordshire; he lived for a very great deal of his life in Olney, in Buckinghamshire, in London and in Huntingdon, but if ever there was a man who took on the texture of East Anglian scenery and East Anglian life it was Cowper. That beautiful river, the Ouse, which empties itself into the Wash, was a peculiar inspiration to Cowper, and those who know the scenery of Olney know that it has conditions exactly analogous in every way to those of East Anglia. One of Cowper's most beautiful poems is entitled "On Receipt of my Mother's Portrait out of Norfolk," and he himself, as I have said, found his last resting-place on East Anglian soil—at East Dereham.

If there may be some doubt about Cowper, there can be none whatever about Edward FitzGerald, the greatest letter-writer of recent times. In mentioning the name of FitzGerald I am a little diffident. It is like introducing "King Charles's head" into this gathering; for was he not the author of the poem known to all of us as the *Rubaiyat of Omar Khayyam*, and there is no small tendency to smile to-day whenever the name of Omar Khayyam is mentioned and to call the cult a "lunacy." It is perhaps unfortunate that FitzGerald gave that somewhat formidable title to his paraphrase, or translation, of the old Persian poet. It is not the fault of those who admire that poem exceedingly that it gives them a suspicion of affecting a scholarship that they do not in most cases possess. What many of us admire is not Omar Khayyam the Persian, nor have we any desire to see or to know any other translation of that poet. We simply admit to an honest appreciation of the poem by Edward FitzGerald, the Suffolk squire, the poem that Tennyson describes as "the one thing done divinely well." That poem by FitzGerald will live as long as the English language, and let it never be forgotten that it is the work of an East Anglian, an East Anglian who, like Borrow, possessed a marked Celtic quality, the outcome of a famous Irish ancestry, nevertheless of an East Anglian who loved its soil, its rivers and its sea.

Then I come to another phase of East Anglian literary traditions. It is astonishing what a zest for learning its women have displayed; I might give you quite a long list of distinguished women who have come out of East Anglia. Crabbe must have had one in mind when he wrote of Arabella in one of his *Tales*:—

> This reasoning maid, above her sex's dread
> Had dared to read, and dared to say she read,
> Not the last novel, not the new born play,
> Not the mere trash and scandal of the day;
> But (though her young companions felt the shock)
> She studied Berkeley, Bacon, Hobbes and Locke.

The one who perhaps made herself most notorious was Harriet Martineau, and in spite of her disagreeable egotism it is still a pleasure to read some of her less controversial writings. Her *Feats on the Fiord*, for example, is really a classic. But I can never quite forgive Harriet Martineau in that she spoke contemptuously of East Anglian scenery, scenery which in its way has charms as great as any part of Europe can offer. No, in this roll of famous women, the two I am most inclined to praise are Sarah Austin and Fanny Burney. Mrs. Austin was, you will remember, one of the Taylors of Norwich, married to John Austin, the famous jurist. She was one of the first to demonstrate that her sex might have other gifts than a gift for writing fiction, and that it was possible to be a good, quiet, domestic woman, and at the same time an exceedingly learned one. Even before Carlyle she gave a vogue to the study of German literature in this country; she wrote many books, many articles, and made some translations, notably what is still the best translation of von Ranke's *History of the Popes*. In the muster-roll of East Anglian worthies let us never forget this singularly good woman, this correspondent of all the most famous men of her day, of Guizot, of Grote, of Gladstone, and one who also, as a letter-writer, showed that she possessed the faculty that seems, as I have said, to be peculiar to the soil of East Anglia. Still less must we forget Fanny Burney, who, born in King's Lynn, lived to delight her own generation by *Evelina* and by the fascinating *Diary* that gives so pleasant a picture of Dr. Johnson and many another of her contemporaries. *Evelina* and the *Diary* are two of my favourite books, but I practise self-restraint and will say no more of them here.

I now come to my ninth, and last, name among those East Anglian worthies whom I feel that we have a particular right to canonize—George Crabbe—"though Nature's sternest painter yet the best," as Byron described him. Now it may be frankly admitted that few of us read Crabbe to-day. He has an acknowledged place in the history of literature, but there pretty well even well-read people are content to leave him. "What have our literary critics been about that they have suffered such a writer to drop into neglect and oblivion?" asks a recent Quarterly Reviewer. He does not live as Cowper does by a few lyrics and ballads and by incomparable letters. Scarcely a line of Crabbe survives in current conversation. If you turn to one of those handy volumes of reference—Dictionaries of Quotation, as they are called—from which we who are journalists are supposed to obtain most of the literary knowledge that we are able to display on occasion, you will scarcely find a dozen lines of Crabbe. And yet I venture to affirm that Crabbe has a great and permanent place in literature, and that as he has been a favourite in the past, he will become a favourite in the future. Crabbe can never lose his place in the history of literature, a place as the forerunner of Wordsworth and even of Cowper, but it would be a tragedy were he to drop out of the category of poets that are read. A dainty little edition in eight volumes is among my most treasured possessions. I have read it not as we read some so-called literature, from a sense of duty, but with unqualified interest. We have had much pure realism in these latter days; why not let us return to the most realistic of the poets. He was beloved by all the greatest among his contemporaries. Scott and Wordsworth were devoted to his work, and so also was Jane Austen. At a later date Tennyson praised him. We have heard quite recently the story of Mr. James Russell Lowell in his last illness finding comfort in reading Scott's *Rob Roy*. Let us turn to Scott's own last illness and see what was the book he most enjoyed, almost on his deathbed:—

"Read me some amusing thing," said Sir Walter, "read me a bit of Crabbe." "I brought out the first volumes of his old favourite that I could lay hand on," says Lockhart, "and turned to what I remembered was one of his favourite passages in it. He listened with great interest. Every now and then he exclaimed, "Capital, excellent, excellent, very good."

Cardinal Newman and Edward FitzGerald at the opposite poles, as it were, of religious impressions, agree in a devotion to Crabbe's poetry. Cardinal Newman speaks of *Tales of the Hall* as "a poem whether in conception or in execution one of the most touching in our language," and in a footnote to his *Idea of a University* he tells us that he had read the poem thirty years earlier with extreme delight, "and have never lost my love of it," and he goes on to plead that it is an absolute *classic*.

Not to have read Crabbe, therefore, is not to know one of the most individual in the glorious muster-roll of English poets, and Crabbe was pre-eminently an East Anglian, born and bred in East Anglia, and taking in a peculiar degree the whole character of his environment, as only Shakspere, Cowper and Wordsworth among our great poets, have done.

In conclusion, let me recapitulate that the names of Marryat, Sir Thomas Browne, George Borrow, Margaret Paston, Horace Walpole, Sarah Austin, Fanny Burney, Edward FitzGerald, and George Crabbe are those that I prefer to associate with East Anglian Literature. We are well aware that literature is but an aspect of our many claims on the gratitude of those Englishmen who have not the good fortune to be East Anglians. We have given to the Empire a great scholar in Porson, a great statesman in Sir Robert Walpole, a great lawyer in Sir Edward Coke, great ecclesiastics in Cardinal Wolsey and Archbishop Parker, great artists in Gainsborough, Constable and Crome, and perhaps above all great sailors in Sir Cloudesley Shovel and the ever memorable Lord Nelson. Personally I admire a certain rebel, Kett the Tanner, as much as any of those I have named.

Of all these East Anglian worthies the praise has often been sung, but let me be pardoned if, on an occasion like this, I have dwelt rather at length on the less familiar association of East Anglia with letters. That I have but touched the fringe of the subject is obvious. What might not be said, for example, concerning Norwich as a literary centre under Bishop Stanley—the Norwich of the Taylors and the Gurneys, possessed of as much real intellectual life as London can boast of to-day. What, again, might not be said of the influence upon writers from afar. Read Kingsley's *Hereward the Wake*, Mr. Swinburne's *Midsummer Holiday*, Charles Dickens' description of Yarmouth and Goldsmith's poetical description in his *Deserted Village*, where clearly Houghton was intended. {153} These, and a host of other memories touch the heart of all good East Anglians, but that East Anglians do not forget the living in doing honour to the dead is indicated by this gathering to-night. We are grateful to Dr. Augustus Jessopp, to Mr. Walter Rye, to Mr. Edward Clodd, and to our guest of this evening, Mr. William Dutt, for keeping alive the folk-lore, the literary history, the historical tradition of that portion of the British Isles to which we feel the most profound attachment by ties of residence or of kinship.

VI

DR. JOHNSON'S ANCESTRY

A paper read before the members of the Johnson Club of London at Simpson's Restaurant in the Strand.

There is, I believe, a definite understanding among our members that we, the Brethren of the Johnson Club, have each and all of us read every line about Dr. Johnson that is in print, to say nothing of his works. It is particularly accepted that the thirteen volumes in which our late brother, Dr. Birkbeck Hill, enshrined his own appreciation of our Great Man, are as familiar to us all as are the Bible and the Book of Common Prayer. For my part, with a deep sense of the responsibility that must belong to any one who has rashly undertaken to read a paper before the Club, I admit to having supplemented these thirteen volumes by a reperusal of the little book entitled *Johnson Club Papers*, by Various Hands, issued in 1899 by Brother Fisher Unwin. I feel as I reread these addresses that there were indeed giants in those days, although my admiration was moderated a little when I came across the statement of one Brother that Johnson's proposal for an edition of Shakspere "came to nothing"; and the statement of another that "Goldsmith's failings were almost as great and as ridiculous as Boswell's;" while my bibliographical ire was awakened by the extraordinary declaration in an article on "Dr. Johnson's Library," that a first folio edition of Shakspere might have realized 250 pounds in the year 1785. Still, I recognize the talent that illuminated the Club in those closing years of the last century. Happily for us, who love good comradeship, most of the giants of those days are still in evidence with their polished armour and formidable spears.

What can I possibly say that has not already been said by one or other of the Brethren? Well, I have put together these few remarks in the hopes that no one of you has seen two books that are in my hands, the first, *The Reades of Blackwood Hill, with Some Account of Dr. Johnson's Ancestry*, by Aleyn Lyell Reade; the other, *The Life and Letters of Dr. Birkbeck Hill*, by his daughter Mrs. Crump. The first of these is privately printed, although it may be bought by any one of the Brethren for a couple of guineas. As far as I am able to learn, Brother Augustine Birrell is the only one of the Brethren who has as yet purchased a copy. The other book, our Brother Birkbeck Hill's biography, is to be issued next week by Mr. Edward Arnold, who has kindly placed an early copy at my disposal. In both these volumes there is much food for reflection for all good Johnsonians. Dr. Johnson's ancestry, it may be, makes little appeal to the crowd, but it will to the Brethren. There is no more favourite subject for satire than the tendency to minute study of an author and his antecedents. But the lover of that author knows the fascination of the topic. He can forgive any amount of zeal. I confess that personally I stand amazed at the variety and interest of Mr. Reade's researches. Let me take a sample case of his method before coming to the main issue. In the opening pages of Boswell's *Johnson* there is some account of Mr. Michael Johnson, the father. The most picturesque anecdote told of Johnson Senior is that concerning a young woman of Leek in Staffordshire, who while he served his apprenticeship there conceived a passion for him, which he did not return. She followed him to Lichfield, where she took lodgings opposite to the house in which he lived, and indulged her hopeless flame. Ultimately she died of love and was buried in the Cathedral at Lichfield, when Michael Johnson put a stone over her grave. This pathetic romance has gone unchallenged by all Boswell's editors, even including our prince of editors, Dr. Birkbeck Hill. Mr. Reade, it seems to me, has completely shattered the story, which, as all Johnsonian students know, was obtained by Boswell from Miss Anna Seward. Mr. Reade is able to show that Michael Johnson had been settled in Lichfield for at least eleven years before the death of Elizabeth Blaney, that for five years she had been the much appreciated domestic in a household in that city. Her will indicates moreover a great affection for her mistress and for that mistress's son; she leaves the boy a gold watch and his mother the rest of her belongings. The only connexion that Michael Johnson would seem to have had with the woman was that he and his brother were called in after her decease to make an inventory of her little property. I think that these little facts about Mistress Blaney, her five years' residence at Lichfield apparently in a most comfortable position, her omission of Michael Johnson from her will, and the fact that he had been in Lichfield at least six months before she arrived, are conclusive.

There is another picturesque fact about Michael Johnson that Mr. Reade has brought to light. It would seem that twenty years before his marriage to Sarah Ford, he had been on the eve of marriage to a young woman at Derby, Mary Neyld; but the marriage did not take place, although the marriage bond was drawn out. Mary was the daughter of Luke Neyld, a prominent tradesman of Derby; she was twenty-three years of age at the time and Michael twenty-nine. Even Mr. Reade's industry has not been able to discover for us why at the very last moment the marriage was broken off. It explains, however, why Michael Johnson married late in life and his melancholia. The human romance that Mr. Reade has unveiled has surely a certain interest for Johnsonians, for had Michael Johnson brought his first love affair to a happy conclusion, we should not have had the man described twenty years later as "possessed of a vile melancholy," who, when his wife's tongue wagged too much, got upon his horse and rode away. There would have been no Samuel Johnson, and there would have been no Johnson Club—a catastrophe which the human mind finds it hard to conceive of. Two years after the breaking off of her engagement with Michael Johnson, I may add, Mary Neyld married one James Warner.

Mr. Reade also calls in question another statement of Boswell's, that Michael Johnson was really apprenticed at Leek in Staffordshire; our only authority for this also is the excellent Anna Seward. Further, it is sufficiently curious that the names of two Samuel Johnsons are recorded as being buried in one of the churches at Lichfield, one before our Samuel came into the world, the other three years later: of these, one died in 1654, the other in 1712. But these points, although of a certain interest, have nothing to do with Dr. Johnson's ancestry. Now before we left our homes this evening, each member of the Johnson Brotherhood, as is his custom, turned up Brother Birkbeck Hill's invaluable index to see what Johnson had to say upon the subject of ancestry. We know that the Doctor was very keen upon the founding of a family; that when Mr. Thrale lost his only son Johnson's sympathies went out to him in a double way, and perhaps in the greater degree because as he said to Boswell, "Sir, don't you know how you yourself think? Sir, he wished to propagate his name." Johnson himself, Boswell tells us, had no pretensions to blood. "I here may say," he said, "that I have great merit in being zealous for subordination and the honours of birth; for I can hardly tell who was my grandfather." Johnson further informed Mrs. Thrale that he did not delight in talking much of his family: "There is little

       Clement Shorter

pleasure," he says, "in relating the anecdotes of beggary." He constantly deprecated his origin. According to Miss Seward, he told his wife before he married her that he was of mean extraction; but the letter in which Miss Seward gives her version of Johnson's courtship is worth recalling, although I do not believe a single word of it:—

The rustic prettiness and artless manners of her daughter, the present Mrs. Lucy Porter, had won Johnson's youthful heart, when she was upon a visit at my grandfather's in Johnson's school-days. Disgusted by his unsightly form, she had a personal aversion to him, nor could the beautiful verses he addressed to her teach her to endure him. The nymph at length returned to her parents at Birmingham, and was soon forgotten. Business taking Johnson to Birmingham on the death of his own father, and calling upon his coy mistress there, he found her father dying. He passed all his leisure hours at Mr. Porter's, attending his sick bed, and in a few months after his death, asked Mrs. Johnson's consent to marry the old widow. After expressing her surprise at a request so extraordinary—"No, Sam, my willing consent you will never have to so preposterous a union. You are not twenty-five, and she is turned fifty. If she had any prudence, this request had never been made to me. Where are your means of subsistence? Porter has died poor, in consequence of his wife's expensive habits. You have great talents, but, as yet, have turned them into no profitable channel." "Mother, I have not deceived Mrs. Porter: I have told her the worst of me; that I am of mean extraction; that I have no money, and that I have had an uncle hanged. She replied, that she valued no one more or less for his descent; that she had no more money than myself; and that, although she had not had a relation hanged, she had fifty who deserved hanging."

Now why did Dr. Johnson take this attitude about his ancestry, so contrary to the spirit that guided him where other people's genealogical trees were concerned? It was certainly not indifference to family ties, because Brother Birkbeck Hill publishes many interesting letters written by Johnson in old age, when finding that he had a certain sum of money to bequeath, he looked around to see if there were any of his own kin living. The number of letters the old man wrote, inquiring for this or that kinsman, are quite pathetic. It seems to me that it was really due to an ignorant vagueness as to his family history. During his early years his family had passed from affluence to penury. They were of a type very common in England, but very rare in Scotland and Ireland, that take no interest whatever in pedigrees, and never discuss any but their immediate relations, with whom, in the case of the Johnsons, very friendly terms did not prevail. I think we should be astonished if we were to go into some shops in London of sturdy prosperous tradesmen in quite as good a position as old Michael Johnson, and were to try and draw out one or other individual upon his ancestry. We should promptly come against a blank wall.

What then do we know of Johnson's father from the ordinary sources? That he was a bookseller at Lichfield, and that he was Sheriff of that city in the year that his son Samuel was born; that he feasted the citizens, as Johnson tells us, in his *Annals*, with "uncommon magnificence." He is described by Johnson as "a foolish old man," because he talked with too fond a pride of his children and their precocious ways. He was a zealous High Churchman and Jacobite. We are told by Boswell further, on the authority of Mr. Hector of Birmingham, that he opened a bookstall once a week in that city, but lost money by setting up as a maker of parchment. "A pious and most worthy man," Mrs. Piozzi tells us of him, "but wrong- headed, positive and affected with melancholia." "I inherited a vile melancholy from my father," Johnson tells us, "which has made me mad all my life." When he died in 1731 his effects were estimated at 20 pounds. "My mother had no value for his relations," Johnson tells us. "Those we knew were much lower than hers." Of Michael Johnson's brother, Andrew, Johnson's uncle, we know still less. From the various Johnson books we only cull the story mentioned in Mrs. Piozzi's *Anecdotes*. She relates that Johnson, after telling her of the prowess of his uncle, Cornelius Ford, at jumping, went on to say that he had another uncle, Andrew—"my father's brother, who kept the ring at Smithfield for a whole year, and was never thrown or conquered. Here are uncles for you, Mistress, if that is the way to your heart." Mr. Reade has supplemented this by showing us that not only was Andrew Johnson a skilful wrestler, but that he was a very good bookseller. For a time he assisted his brother in the conduct of the business at Lichfield. Later, however, he settled as a bookseller at Birmingham, which was to be his home until his death over thirty years later. Here he published some interesting books; the title- pages of some of these are given by Mr. Reade, who reproduces of course his will. He had a son named Thomas who fell on evil days. You will find certain letters to Thomas in Birkbeck Hill's edition; Dr. Johnson frequently helped him with money.

Of more interest, however, than Andrew Johnson was Catherine, the one sister of Michael and Andrew, an aunt of Samuel's, who was evidently for some unknown reason ignored by her two brothers. Here we are not on absolutely firm ground, but it seems to me clear that Catherine Johnson married into a position far above her brothers. A fortnight before his death Dr. Johnson wrote to the Rev. William Vyse, Rector of Lambeth; a letter in which he asked him to find out "whether Charles Skrymsher"—he misspelt it "Scrimshaw"— "of Woodseaves"—he misspelt it "Woodease"—"in your neighbourhood, be now alive," and whether he could be found without delay. He added that "it will be an act of great kindness to me," Charles Skrymsher being "very nearly related." Charles Skrymsher was not found, and Johnson told Dr. Vyse that he was disappointed in the inquiries that he had made for his relations. This particular relation, indeed, had been twenty-two years dead when Dr. Johnson, probably with the desire of leaving him something in his will, made these inquiries. His mother, Mrs. Gerald Skrymsher, was Michael Johnson's sister. One of her daughters became the wife of Thomas Boothby. Boothby was twice married, and his two wives were cousins, the first, Elizabeth, being the daughter of one Sir Charles Skrymsher, the second, Hester, as I have said, of Gerald Skrymsher, Dr. Johnson's uncle. Hence Johnson had a cousin by marriage who was a potentate in his day, for it is told of Thomas Boothby of Tooley Park, grand-nephew of a powerful and wealthy baronet, that he was one of the fathers of English sport. An issue of *The Field* newspaper for 1875 contains an engraving of a hunting horn then in the possession of the late Master of the Cheshire Hounds, and upon the horn is the inscription: "Thomas Boothby, Esq., Tooley Park, Leicester. With this horn he hunted the first pack of fox hounds then in England fifty-five years." He died in 1752. His eldest son took the maternal name of Skrymsher, and under the title of Thomas Boothby Skrymsher became M.P. for Leicester, and an important person in his day. His wife was Anne, daughter of Sir Hugh Clopton of New Place, Stratford-on-Avon. Admirers of Mrs. Gaskell will remember the Clopton legend told by her in Howett's *Visits to Remarkable Places*.

I wish that I had time to follow Mr. Reade through all the ramifications of an interesting family history, but I venture to think that there is something pathetic in Dr. Johnson's inquiries a fortnight before his death as to cousins of whose life story he knew nothing, whose well-known family home of Woodseaves he—the great Lexicographer—could not spell correctly, and of whose very name he was imperfectly informed. Yet he, the lover of family trees and of ancestral associations, was all his life in ignorance of these wealthy connexions and their many substantial intermarriages.

Before Mr. Reade it was known that Johnson's father was a manufacturer of parchment as well as a bookseller; but it was supposed that only in his last few years or so of life did he undertake this occupation which ruined him. Mr. Reade shows that he had been for thirty years engaged in this trade in parchment. Brother Birkbeck Hill quotes Croker, who hinted that Johnson's famous definition of Excise as "a hateful tax levied upon commodities, and adjudged not by the Common Judge of Property but by wretches hired by those to whom Excise is paid," was inspired by recollections of his father's constant disputes with the Excise officers. Mr. Reade has unearthed documents concerning the crisis of this quarrel, when Michael Johnson in 1718 was indicted "for useing ye Trade of a Tanner." The indictment, which is here printed in full, charges him, "one Michael Johnson, bookseller," "that he did in the third year of the reign of our Lord George by the Grace of God now King of Great Britain, for his own proper gain, get up, use and exercise the art, mystery or manual occupation of a Byrseus, in English a Tanner, in which art, mystery or manual occupation of a Tanner the said Michael Johnson was not brought up or apprenticed for the space of seven years, an evil example of all others offending in such like case." Michael's defence was that he was "tanned for" and did not tan himself, he being only "a merchant in skins tradeing to Ireland, Scotland and the furthermost parts of England." The only known example of Michael Johnson's handwriting is this defence. Michael was committed for trial but acquitted. It is probable, however, that this prosecution laid the foundation of his ruin.

But I must pass on to the other branch: the family of Dr.

Johnson's mother. Here Dr. Johnson did himself a great injustice, for he had a genuine right to count his mother's "an old family," although the term is in any case relative. At any rate he could carry his pedigree back to 1620. "In the morning," says Boswell, "we had talked of old families, and the respect due to them. Johnson said—

> "'Sir, you have a right to that kind of respect, and are arguing for yourself. I am for supporting the principle, and I am disinterested in doing it, as I have no such right.'"

Nevertheless, Boswell, in this opening chapter, refers to the mother as "Sarah Ford, descended of an ancient race of substantial yeomanry in Warwickshire," and Johnson's epitaph upon his mother's tomb describes her as "of the ancient family of Ford." Thus one is considerably bewildered in attempting to reconcile Johnson's attitude. The only one of his family for whom he seems to have had a good word was Cornelius Harrison, of whom, writing to Mrs. Thrale, he said that he was "perhaps the only one of my relations who ever rose in fortune above penury or in character above neglect." This Cornelius was the son of John Harrison, who had married Johnson's aunt, Phoebe Ford. Johnson's account of Uncle John in his *Annals* is not flattering, but he was the son of a Rector of Pilborough, whose father was Sir Richard Harrison, one of the gentlemen of the King's Bedchamber, and a personality of a kind. Cornelius, the reputable cousin, died in 1748, but his descendants seem to have been a poor lot, whatever his ancestors may have been. Mr. Reade traces their history with all the relentlessness of the genealogist.

Johnson's great-grandfather was one Henry Ford, a yeoman in Birmingham. One of his sons, Henry, Johnson's grand-uncle, was born in 1628. He owned property at West Bromwich and elsewhere, and was a fellow of Clifford's Inn, London. Then we come to Cornelius Ford—"Cornelius Ford, gentleman," he is styled in his marriage settlement. Cornelius died four months before Samuel Johnson was born. Cornelius had a sister Mary, who married one Jesson, and their only son, I may mention incidentally, entered at Pembroke College in 1666, sixty years before his second-cousin, our Samuel, entered the same college. Another cousin by marriage was a Mrs. Harriots, to whom Johnson refers in his *Annals*, and also in his *Prayers and Meditations*. The only one of Cornelius Ford's family referred to in the biographies is Joseph Ford, the father of the notorious Parson Ford, Johnson's cousin, of whom he several times speaks. Joseph was a physician of eminence who settled at Stourbridge. He married a wealthy widow, Mrs. Hickman. He was a witness to the marriage of his sister Sarah to Michael Johnson. There can be no doubt but that the presence of Dr. Ford and his family at Stourbridge accounts for Johnson being sent there to school in 1725. He stayed in the house of his cousin Cornelius Ford, not as Boswell says his *uncle* Cornelius, at Pedmore, about a mile from Stourbridge. He walked in every day to the Grammar School. A connexion of the boy, Gregory Hickman, was residing next to the Grammar School. A kinsman of Johnson and a descendant of Hickman, Dr. Freer, still lives in the house. I met him at Lichfield recently, and he has sent me a photograph of the very house, which stands to-day much as it did when Johnson visited it, and wrote at twenty-two, a sonnet to Dorothy Hickman "playing at the Spinet." Dorothy was one of Johnson's three early loves, with Ann Hector and Olivia Lloyd. Dorothy married Dr. John Turtin and had an only child, Dr. Turtin, the celebrated physician who attended Goldsmith in his last illness.

I have not time to go through the record of all Dr. Johnson's uncles on the maternal side, and do full justice to Mr. Reade's industry and mastery of detail. I may, however, mention incidentally that the uncle who was hanged, if one was, must have been one of his father's brothers, for to the Fords that distinction does not seem to have belonged. Much that is entertaining is related of the cousin Parson Ford, who, after sharing with the famous Earl of Chesterfield in many of his profligacies, received from his lordship the Rectory of South Luffenham. There is no evidence, however, that Chesterfield ever knew that his at one time chaplain and boon companion was cousin of the man who wrote him the most famous of letters.

The mother of Cornelius Ford was a Crowley, and this brings Johnson into relationship with London city worthies, for Mrs. Ford's brother was Sir Ambrose Crowley, Kt., Alderman, of London, the original of Addison's Jack Anvil. One of Sir Ambrose Crowley's daughters married Humphrey Parsons, sometime M.P. for London and twice Lord Mayor. Thus we see that during the very years of Johnson's most painful struggle in London one of his distant cousins or connexions was Chief Magistrate of this City. Another connexion, Elizabeth Crowley, was married in 1724 at Westminster Abbey to John, tenth Lord St. John of Bletsoe. "Here are ancestors for you, Mistress," Dr. Johnson might have said to Mrs. Thrale if he had only known—if he had had a genealogist at his elbow as well as a pushful biographer.

Mr. Reade prints the whole of the marriage settlement upon the union of Johnson's mother and father. It is a very elaborate document, and suggests the undoubted prosperity of the parties at the time. The husband was fifty, the bride thirty-seven. Samuel was not born until three years and three months after the marriage. The pair frequently in early married life received assistance by convenient deaths as the following extracts from wills indicate:—

Cornelius Ford of Packwood in the Co. of Warwick.

I give and bequeath unto my son-in-law Michaell Johnson the sum of five pounds, and to his wife my daughter five and twenty pounds.

Proved May 1, 1709.

Jane Ford of Old Turnford, widow of Joseph Ford.

I do will and appoint that my son Cornelius Ford do and shall pay to my brother-in-law, Mr. Michael Johnson and his wife and their trustees, the sum of 200 pounds which is directed by his late father's Will to be paid to me and in lieu of so much moneys which my said late husband received in trust for my said brother Johnson and his wife.

Proved at Worcester, October 2, 1722.

Then "good cousin Harriotts" does not forget them:—

I give and bequeath to my cousin Sarah the wife of Michael Johnson the like sum of 40 pounds for her own separate use, and one pair of my best flaxen sheets and pillow coats, a large pewter dish and a dozen of pewter plates, provided that her husband doth at the same time give the like bond to my executor to permit his wife to dispose of the same at her will and pleasure.

Elizabeth Harriotts of Trysall in Staff.,
October 23, 1726.

But I must leave this fascinating volume. I cannot find time to tell you all it has to say about the Porter family. Mr. Reade is as informative when treating of the Porters, of Mrs. Johnson and her daughter Lucy, as he is with the family trees of which I have spoken.

I hasten on to Dr. Hill's *Life*, with which I am only concerned here at the point where it is affected by Mr. Reade's book. The reflection inevitably arises that it is well-nigh impossible efficiently to do work involving research unless one has an income derived from other sources. Your historian in proportion to the value of his work must be a rich man, and so must the biographer. Good as Brother Birkbeck Hill's work was, it would have been better if he had had more money. He might have had many of these wills and other documents copied, upon the securing of which Mr. Reade must have expended such very large sums. Dr. Hill was fully alive to this. "If I had not some private means," he wrote to a friend in 1897, "I could never edit Johnson and Boswell; but I do not get so well paid as a carpenter." As a matter of fact, I find that he lost exactly 3 pounds by publishing *Dr. Johnson: his Friends and his Critics*. He made 320 pounds by the first four years' sale of the "Boswell." This 320 pounds, including American rights, made the bulk of his payments for his many years' work, and the book has not yet gone into a second edition. I think 2,000 were printed. There were between 40,000 and 50,000 copies of Croker's editions sold, so that we must not be too boastful as to the improved taste of the present age. 320 pounds is a mere bagatelle to numbers of our present writers of utterly foolish fiction. Several of them have been known to spend double that sum on a single motor-car. In connexion with this matter I cannot refrain from giving one passage from a letter of Brother Hill's:—

My old friend D—lamented that the two new volumes (of my *Johnson Miscellanies*) are so dear as to be above his reach. The net price is a guinea. On Sunday he had eight glasses of hollands and seltzer—a shilling each, a pint of stout and some cider, besides half a dozen cigars or so. Two days' abstinence from cigars and liquor would have paid for my book.

Mrs. Crump, who writes her father's life, has expressed regret to me that there is so little in the book concerning the Johnson Club to which Brother Hill was so devoted. She had asked me for letters, but I felt that all in my possession were unsuited for publication, dealing rather freely with living persons. Brother Hill was impatient of the mere book-maker—the literary charlatan who wrote without reading sufficiently. There are two pleasant glimpses of our Club in the volume; I quote one. It was of the night that we discussed *Dr. Johnson as a Radical*:—

I wish that you and Lucy could have been present last night and witnessed my scene of triumph. I was indeed most nobly welcomed. The scribe told me with sympathetic pride that the correspondent of the *New York Herald* had asked leave to attend, as he wished to telegraph my paper out to America!!! as well as the discussion. There were some very good speeches made in the discussion that followed, especially by a Mr. Whale, a solicitor, who spoke remarkably well and with great knowledge of his *Boswell*. He said that he preferred to call it, not Johnson's radical side, but his humanitarian side. Mr. Birrell, the *Obiter Dicta* man, also spoke very well. He is a clever fellow. He was equally compli-mentary. He maintained in opposition to Mr. Whale that radical was the right term, and in fact that radicalism and humanitarianism were the same. Many of them said what a light the paper had thrown on Johnson's character. One gentleman came up and congratulated me on the very delicate way in which I had handled so difficult a subject, and had not given offence to the Liberal Unionists and Tories present. Edmund Gosse, by whom I sat, was most friendly, and called the paper a wonderful *tour de force*, referring to the way in which I had linked Johnson's sayings. He asked me to visit him some day at Trinity College, Cambridge, and assured me of a hearty welcome.

It is no wonder that what with the supper and the smoke I did not get to sleep till after two. Among the guests was the great Bonner, the Australian cricketer, whose health had been drunk with that of the other visitors, and his praise sounded at having hit some balls over the pavilion at Lord's. With great simplicity he said that after seeing the way in which Johnson's memory was revered, he would much rather have been such a man than have gained his own greatest triumphs at cricket. He did not say it jocularly at all.

Another letter from Dr. Hill describes how he found himself at Ashbourne in Derbyshire with the Club, or rather with a fragment of it. He wrote from the *Green Man* there concerning his adventures.

I have far exceeded my time, but I would like in conclusion to say how admirably his daughter has written this book on our Brother Birkbeck Hill. What a pleasant picture it presents of a genuine lover of literature. His was not an analytical mind nor was he a great critic. His views on Dante and Newman will not be shared by any of us. But, what is far more important than analysis or criticism, he had an entirely lovable personality and was a most clubbable man. He was moreover the ideal editor of Boswell. What more could be said in praise of a beloved Brother of the Johnson Club!

VII

THE PRIVATE LIFE OF
FERDINAND LASSALLE {185}

Ich habe die Inventur meines Lebens gemacht.
Es war gross, brav, wacker, tapfer und glanzend genug.
Eine kunftige Zeit wird mir gerecht zu warden wissen.

—FERDINAND LASSALLE, *August* 9, 1864.

I. The Countess Sophie von Hatzfeldt.

Ferdinand Lassalle was born at Breslau on April 11, 1825.
His parents were of Jewish race, his father a successful silk
merchant. From boyhood he was now the tyrant, now the
slave of a mother whom he loved and by whom he was
adored. Heymann Lassal—his son changed the spelling
during his Paris sojourn—appears to have been irritable and
tyrannical; and there are some graphic instances in the
recently published "Diary" {186} of the differences between
them, ending on one occasion in the boy rushing to the river,
where his terrified father finds him hesitating on the brink,
and becomes reconciled. A more attractive picture of the old
man is that told of his visit to his son-in-law, Friedland, who

had married Lassalle's sister. Friedland was ashamed of his Jewish origin, and old Lassalle startled the guests at dinner by rising and frankly stating that he was a Jew, that his daughter was a Jewess, and that her husband was of the same race. The guests cheered, but the host never forgave his too frank father-in-law.

Lassalle was a student at Breslau University, and later at Berlin, where he laid the foundation of those Hegelian studies to which he owed his political philosophy. In 1845 he went to Paris, and there secured the friendship of Heine, being included with George Sand in the interesting circle around the "mattress grave" of the sick poet.

Among Heine's letters {187} there are four addressed to Lassalle, now as "Dear and best beloved friend," now as "Dearest brother-in-arms." "Be assured," he says, "that I love you beyond measure. I have never before felt so much confidence in any one." "I have found in no one," he says again, "so much passion and clearness of intellect united in action. You have good right to be audacious—we others only usurp this Divine right, this heavenly privilege." And to Varnhagen von Ense he writes:—

> My friend, Herr Lassalle, who brings you this letter, is a young man of the most remarkable intellectual gifts. With the most thorough erudition, with the widest learning, with the greatest penetration that I have ever known, and with the richest gift of exposition, he combines an energy of will and a capacity for action which astonish me. . . . In no one have I found united so much enthusiasm and practical intelligence.

"In every line," says Brandes, "this letter shows the far-seeing student of life, indeed, the prophet!"

Clement Shorter

Lassalle is not backward in reciprocating the enthusiasm.

"I love Heine," he declares; "he is my second self. What audacity! what crushing eloquence! He knows how to whisper like a zephyr when it kisses rose-blooms, how to breathe like fire when it rages and destroys; he calls forth all that is tenderest and softest, and then all that is fiercest and most daring. He has the command of all the range of feeling."

Lassalle's sympathy with Heine never lessened. It was Heine who lost grasp of the intrinsically higher nature of his countryman and co-religionist, and an acute difference occurred, as we shall see, when Lassalle interfered in the affairs of the Countess von Hatzfeldt. Introduced to the Countess by his friend Dr. Mendelssohn, in 1846, Lassalle felt that here in concrete form was scope for all his enthusiasm of humanity, and he determined to devote his life to championing the cause of the oppressed lady. {188} The Countess was the wife of a wealthy and powerful nobleman, who ill-treated her shamefully. He imprisoned her in his castles, refused her doctors and medicine in sickness, and carried off her children. Her own family, as powerful as the Count, had often intervened, and the Count's repentances were many but short-lived. In 1846 matters reached a crisis. The Count wrote to his second son, Paul, asking him to leave his mother. The boy carried this letter to the Countess; and Lassalle relates that, finding the lady in tears, he persuaded her to a full disclosure of the facts. He pledged himself to save her, and for nine years carried on the struggle, with ultimate victory, but with considerable loss of reputation. He first told the story to Mendelssohn and Oppenheim, two friends of great wealth, the latter a Judge of one of the superior courts in Prussia. They agreed to help him; for then, as always, Lassalle's persuasive powers were irresistible. They went with him from Berlin to Dusseldorf, the Count being in that neighbourhood. Von Hatzfeldt was at Aix-la-Chapelle, caught in the toils of a new mistress, the Baroness Meyendorff. Lassalle discovered that she had obtained from the Count a deed assigning to her some property which should in the ordinary course have come to the boy Paul. The Countess, hearing of the disaster which seemed likely to befall her favourite son, made her way into her husband's presence, and in the scene which followed secured a promise that the document should be revoked—destroyed. But no sooner had she left him than the Count returned to the Meyendorff influence, and refused to see his wife again. Soon afterwards it was discovered that the woman had set out for Cologne. Lassalle begged his friends Oppenheim and Mendelssohn, to follow her and, if possible, to ascertain whether the momentous document had actually been destroyed. They obeyed, and reached the hotel at Cologne about the same time as the Baroness. Here they were guilty of an indiscretion, if of nothing worse, for which Lassalle can surely in no way be blamed, but which was used for many a year to tarnish his name. Oppenheim, on his way upstairs, observed a servant with the luggage of the Baroness; among other things a desk or casket of a kind commonly used to carry valuable papers. Thinking only of the fact that it was desirable to obtain a certain document from the brutal Count, he pounced upon the casket when the servant's back was turned. But he had no luggage with him in which to conceal it, and so handed it to Mendelssohn. Mendelssohn, although fully sensible of the blunder that had been committed, could not desert his friend, and placed the casket in his trunk.

The whole hotel was in an uproar when the Baroness discovered her loss. The friends fled panic-stricken in opposite directions. Suspicion immediately fell upon Dr. Mendelssohn, because his room was seen to have been left in confusion. He was pursued, but succeeded in escaping from a railway carriage and fleeing to Paris, leaving his luggage in the hands of the police. In his box some papers were found which incriminated Oppenheim; and Oppenheim, a Judge of one of the superior courts, and the son of a millionaire, was arrested and imprisoned for theft!

Lassalle visited Oppenheim in prison, and extracted from him a promise of silence as to the motive for his conduct. He then threw himself vigorously into the struggle, both in the press and in the law courts. Here he seems to have parted company with Heine, because, as he tells us, "the Baroness Meyendorff was a friend of the Princess de Lieven, and the Princess de Lieven was the mistress of Guizot, and Heine received a pension from Guizot."

Oppenheim was acquitted in 1846, and Mendelssohn, who was really innocent of the actual robbery, naturally thought it safe to return to Germany. He was, however, tried before the assize court of Cologne, and sentenced to five years' imprisonment. Alexander von Humboldt obtained a reduction of the sentence to one year, but on condition that Mendelssohn should leave Europe. He went, after his release from prison, to Constantinople, and when the Crimean war broke out joined the Turkish army, dying on the march in 1854.

Meanwhile Germany rang for many years with the story of the so-called robbery, and Lassalle's name was even more associated therewith than were those of his more culpable friends. And this was not unnatural, because he was engaged year after year in continuous warfare with Count Hatzfeldt. At length, in 1854, about the time that the unfortunate Dr. Mendelssohn died in the East, he secured for the Countess complete separation and an ample provision.

Lassalle's friendship with this lady inevitably gave rise to scandal. But never surely was scandal so little justified. She was twenty years his senior, and the relation was clearly that of mother and son. In her letters he is always "my dear child," and in his she is the confidante of the innumerable troubles of mind and of heart of which so impressionable a man as Ferdinand Lassalle had more than his share.

"You are without reason and judgment where women are concerned," she tells him, when he confides to her his passion for Helene von Donniges; and the remark opens out a vista of confidences of which the world happily knows but little. From the assize court of Dusseldorf, of all places, we have a very definite glimpse of a good-looking man, likely to be a favourite in the society of the opposite sex:—

> "Ferdinand Lassalle," runs the official document, "aged twenty-three, a civilian, born at Breslau, and dwelling recently at Berlin. Stands five feet six inches in height, has brown curly hair, open forehead, brown eyebrows, dark blue eyes, well proportioned nose and mouth, and rounded chin."

He was indeed a favourite in Berlin drawing-rooms, pronounced a "Wunderkind" by Humboldt, and enthusiastically admired on all sides. But, assuming the story of Sophie Solutzeff to be mythical, there is no evidence that Lassalle had ever had any very serious romance in his life until he met Helene von Donniges.

Es ist eine alte Geschichte,
Doch bleibt sie immer neu.—HEINE.

II. Helene von Donniges

Helene von Donniges has told us the story in fullest detail—the story of that tragic love which was to send Lassalle to his too early death. She was the daughter of a Bavarian diplomatist who had held appointments in Italy, and later in Switzerland. She was betrothed as a child of twelve to an Italian of forty years of age. At a time when, as she says, her thoughts should have been concentrated upon her studies, they were distracted by speculations on marriage and the marriage tie. A young Wallachian student named Yanko Racowitza crossed her path. His loneliness—he was far from home and friends—kindled her sympathy. Dark and ugly, she compared him to Othello, and called him her "Moor." In spite of some parental opposition she insisted upon plighting her troth to him, and the Italian lover was scornfully dismissed. Then comes the opening scene of the present story. It was in Berlin, whither Helen—we will adopt the English spelling of the name—had travelled with her grandmother in 1862, that she was asked at a ball the momentous question, "Do you know Lassalle?" She had never heard his name. Her questioner was Baron Korff, a son-in-law of Meyerbeer, who, charmed by her originality, remarked that she and Lassalle were made for one another. Two weeks later her curiosity was further excited, when Dr. Karl Oldenberg let fall some similar remark as to her intellectual kinship with the mysterious Lassalle. She asked her grandmother about him, and was told that he was a "shameless demagogue." Then she turned to her lover, who promised to inquire. Racowitza brought her information about the Countess, the casket, and other "sensations"—only to excite her curiosity the more. Finally a friend, Frau Hirsemenzel, undertook to introduce her to the notorious Socialist. The introduction took place at a party, and if her account is to be trusted, no romance could be more dramatic than the actuality. They loved one another at first sight, conversed with freedom, and he called her by an endearing name as he offered her his arm to escort her home.

"Somehow it did not seem at all remarkable," she says, "that a stranger should thus call me 'Du' on first acquaintance. We seemed to fit to one another so perfectly."

She was in her nineteenth year, Lassalle in his thirty-ninth. The pair did not see one another again for some months, not in fact until Helen visited Berlin as the guest of a certain lawyer Holthoff. Here she met Lassalle at a concert, and the friendly lawyer connived at their being more than once together. At a ball, on one occasion, Lassalle asked her what she would do if he were sentenced to death, and she beheld him ascending the scaffold.

"I should wait till your head was severed," was her answer, "in order that you might look upon your beloved to the last, and then—I should take poison."

He was pleased with her reply, but declared that there was no fear—his star was in the ascendant! And so it seemed; for although young Racowitza even then accosted him in the ballroom, the friendly Holthoff soon arranged an informal betrothal; and Lassalle was on the eve of a great public triumph which seemed more likely to take him to the throne than to the scaffold.

To many this will seem an exaggeration. Yet hear Prince Bismarck in the Reichstag seventeen years after Lassalle's death:—

He was one of the most intellectual and gifted men with whom I have ever had intercourse, a man who was ambitious in high style, but who was by no means

Republican: he had very decided national and monarchical sympathies, and the idea which he strove to realize was the German Empire, and therein we had a point of contact. Lassalle was extremely ambitious, and it was perhaps a matter of doubt to him whether the German Empire would close with the Hohenzollern dynasty or the Lassalle dynasty; but he was monarchical through and through. Lassalle was an energetic and very intellectual man, to talk with whom was very instructive. Our conversations lasted for hours, and I was always sorry when they came to an end. {198}

The year 1864, which was to close so tragically, opened indeed with extraordinary promise. Lassalle left Berlin in May—Helen had gone back to Geneva two or three months earlier—travelling by Leipzig and Cologne through the Rhenish provinces, and holding a "glorious review" the while.

"I have never seen anything like it," he writes to the Countess von Hatzfeldt. "The entire population indulged in indescribable jubilation. The impression made upon me was that such scenes must have attended the founding of new religions."

And it appeared possible that Heine's description of Lassalle as the Messiah of the nineteenth century was to be realized. The Bishop of Mayence was on his side, and the King of Prussia sympathetic. As he passed from town to town the whole population turned out to do him honour. Countless thousands met him at the stations: the routes were ornamented with triumphal arches, the houses decorated with wreaths, and flowers were thrown upon him as he passed. As the cavalcade approached the town of Ronsdorf, for example, it was easy to see that the people were on tip-toe with expectation. At the entrance an arch bore the inscription:—

Willkommen dem Dr. Ferdinand Lassalle
Viel tausendmal im Ronsdorfer Thal!

Under arches and garlands, smothered with flowers thrown by young work- girls, whose fathers, husbands, brothers, cheered again and again, Lassalle and his friends entered the town, while a vast multitude followed in procession. It was at Ronsdorf that Lassalle made the speech which had in it something of fateful presentiment:—

"I have not grasped this banner," he said, "without knowing quite clearly that I myself may fall. The feelings which fill me at the thought that I may be removed cannot be better expressed than in the words of the Roman poet:

'*Exoriare aliquis nostris ex ossibus ultor!*'

or in German, '*Moge, wenn ich beseitigt werde, irgend ein Racher und Nachfolger aus meinen Gebeinen auferstehen!*' May this great and national movement of civilization not fall with my person, but may the conflagration which I have kindled spread farther and farther, so long as one of you still breathes. Promise me that, and in token raise your right hands."

All hands were raised in silence, and the impressive scene closed with a storm of acclamation.

But Lassalle was worn out, and he fled for a time from the storm and conflict to Switzerland. Helen at Geneva heard of his sojourn at Righi-Kaltbad, and she made an excursion thither with two or three friends, and thus on July 25 (1864) the lovers met again. An account of their romantic interview comes to us in Helen's own diary and in the letter which Lassalle wrote to the Countess Hatzfeldt two days later. Helen tells how they climbed the Kulm together, discussing

Clement Shorter

by the way the question of their marriage and the possibility of opposition.

"What have your parents against me?" asked Lassalle; and was told that only once had she mentioned his name before them, and that their horror of the Jew agitator had ever since closed her mouth. So the conversation sped. The next morning their hope of "a sunrise" was destroyed by a fog. "How often," says Helen, "when in later years I have stood upon the summit of the Righi and seen the day break in all its splendour, have I recalled this foggy, damp morning, and Lassalle's disappointment!"

As he looked upon her, so pale and trembling, he abused the climate, and promised that he would give up politics, devote himself to science and literature, and take her to Egypt or India. He talked to her of the Countess, "who will think only of my happiness," and he talked of religion. Was his Jewish faith against him in her eyes? Mahommedanism and Judaism, it was all one to her, was the answer, but paganism by preference! They parted, to correspond immediately, and Lassalle to write to the astonished, and in this affair, unsympathetic Countess, of the meeting with his beloved. With the utmost friendliness, however, he endeavoured to keep the elder lady at a distance for a time.

On July 20 Helen writes to him, repeating her promise to become his wife.

You said to me yesterday: "Say but a sensible and decided 'Yes'—*et je me charge du reste.*" Good; I say "Yes"—*chargez-vous donc du reste.* I only require that we first do all in our power to win my parents to a friendly attitude. To me belongs, however, a painful task. I must slay in cold blood the true heart of Yanko von Racowitza, who has given me the purest love, the noblest devotion. With heartless egotism I must destroy the day-dream of a noble youth. But for your sake I will even do what is wrong.

Meanwhile Lassalle's unhappy attempts to conciliate the Countess continue. He writes of Helen's sympathy and dwells upon her entire freedom from jealousy. He tells Frau von Hatzfeldt how much Helen is longing to see his old friend. In conclusion, as though not to show himself too blind a lover, he remarks that Helen's one failing is a total lack of will. "When, however, we are man and wife," he adds, "then shall I have 'will' enough for both, and she will be as clay in the hands of the potter." The Countess continues obdurate, and in a further letter (Aug. 2) Lassalle says:—

It is really a piece of extraordinary good fortune that, at the age of thirty-nine and a half, I should be able to find a wife so beautiful, so sympathetic, who loves me so much, and who—an indispensable requirement—is so entirely absorbed in my personality.

At Lassalle's request, Helen herself wrote thus to the Baroness von Hatzfeldt:—

DEAR AND BELOVED COUNTESS,—

Armed with an introduction from my lord and master, I, his affianced wife, come to you—unhappily only in writing—*le coeur et la main ouverte*, and beg of you a little of that friendship which you have given to him so abundantly. How deeply do I regret that your illness separates us, that I cannot tell you face to face how much I love and honour him, how ardently I long for your help and advice as to how I can best make my beautiful and noble eagle happy. This my first letter must necessarily seem somewhat constrained to you; for I am an insignificant, unimportant being, who can do nothing but love and honour him, and strive to make him happy. I would fain dance and sing like a child, and drive away all care from him. My one desire is to understand his great and noble nature, and in good fortune and in bad to stand faithful and true by his side.

Then followed a further appeal for the love and help of this friend of Lassalle's early years. It was all in vain. Instead of a letter, Helen received from the Countess what she called "a scrawl," and Lassalle a long homily on his lack of judgment and foresight. Lassalle defended himself, and so the not too pleasing correspondence went on.

Yet these days in Berne were the happiest in the lives of Lassalle and his betrothed. Helen was staying with a Madame Aarson, and was constantly visited by her lover. It was agreed between them that Lassalle should follow her to Geneva, and see her parents. But no sooner had he entered his room at the Pension Leovet, in the neighbourhood of the house of Herr von Donniges, than a servant handed him a letter from Helen. It told how on her arrival she had found the whole house excited by the betrothal of her sister Margaret to Count von Keyserling. Her mother's delight in the engagement had tempted her (contrary to Lassalle's express wish) to confidences, and she had told of her love for the arch-agitator. Her mother had turned upon her with loathing, execrated Lassalle without stint, spoken scornfully of the Countess, the casket robbery, and kindred matters. "It is quite impossible," urged the frantic woman, "that Count Keyserling will unite himself to a family with a connexion of this kind." The father joined in the upbraiding, the disowning of an undutiful daughter. One has but to remember the vulgar, tradesman instinct, which then, as now, guides the marriage ideals of a certain class, to take in the whole situation at a glance.

Lassalle had hardly begun to read the letter when Helen appeared before him, and begged him to take her away immediately—to France—anywhere! Her father's violence, her mother's abuse, had driven her to despair.

Lassalle was indignant with her. Why had she not obeyed him? He would speak to her father. All would yet be well. But—she was compromised there—at his hotel. Had she a friend in the neighbourhood?

At this moment her maid came in to say that there was a carriage ready to take them to the station. A train would start for Paris in a quarter of an hour. Helen renewed her entreaty, but Lassalle remained resolute. He would only receive her from her father. To what friend could he take her? Helen named Madame Caroline Rognon, who beheld them with astonishment.

A few minutes later Frau von Donniges and her daughter Margaret entered the house. Then followed a disagreeable scene between Lassalle and the mother, ending, after many scornful words thrown at the ever self-restrained lover, in Helen being carried off before his eyes—indeed, by his wish. Lassalle had shown dignity and self-restraint, but he had killed the girl's love—until it was too late.

Duhring speaks of Lassalle's "inconceivable stupidity," and there is a great temptation at this date, with all the circumstances before us, to look at the matter with Duhring's eyes. But to one whom Heine had called a Messiah, whom Humboldt had termed a "Wunderkind," and Bismarck had greeted as among the greatest men of the age, it may well have seemed flatly inconceivable that this insignificant little Swiss diplomatist could long refuse the alliance he proposed. Yet stronger and more potent may have been the feeling— although of this there is no positive evidence extant—that the

Clement Shorter

social movement which he had so much at heart could not well endure a further scandal. The Hatzfeldt story had been used against him frequently enough. An elopement—so sweetly romantic under some circumstances—would have been the ruin of his great political reputation.

Lassalle speedily regretted his course of action—what man in love would not have done so?—but his first impulse was consistent with the life of strenuous effort for the cause he had embraced. To a romantic girl, however, his conduct could but seem brutal and treacherous. Helen had done more than enough. She had compromised herself irretrievably, and an immediate marriage was imperatively demanded by the conventionalities. She was, however, seized by a brutal father and confined to her room, until she understood that Lassalle had left Geneva. Then the entreaties of her family, the representation that her sister's marriage, even her father's position, were in jeopardy, caused her to declare that she would abandon Lassalle.

At this point the story is conflicting. Helen herself says that she never saw Lassalle again after he had handed her over to her mother, and that after a long period of ill-usage and petty persecution, she was hurried one night across the lake. Becker, however, declares that as Lassalle and his friend Rustow were walking in Geneva a carriage passed them on the way to the station containing Helen and another lady, and that Helen acknowledged their salute. Anyway, it is clear that Helen went to Bex on August 9, and that Lassalle left Geneva on the 13th. Letter after letter was sent by Lassalle to Helen—one from Karlsruhe on the 15th, and one from Munich on the 19th, but no answer. In Karlsruhe, according to von Hofstetten, Lassalle wept like a child. His correspondence with the Countess and with Colonel Rustow becomes forcible in its demands for assistance. Writing to Rustow, he tells of a two hours' conversation with the

Bavarian Minister for Foreign Affairs, Baron von Schrenk, who assures him of his sympathy, says that he cannot understand the objections of von Donniges, and that in similar circumstances he would be proud of the alliance, although he deprecated the political views of Lassalle. Finally this accommodating Minister of State—here, at least, the tragi-comedy is but too apparent—engages to send a lawyer, Dr. Haenle, as an official commissioner to negotiate with the obdurate father and refractory ambassador.

Richard Wagner, the great composer, the Bishop of Mayence, and noblemen, generals, and scholars without number were also pressed into the service, but in vain. The treachery of intimate friends more than counterbalanced all that could be achieved by well-meaning strangers. If Helen is to be believed—and the charge is not denied—Lassalle's friend Holthoff, sent to negotiate in his favour, entreated her to abandon Lassalle, and to comply with her parents' wishes. Lassalle, he declared, was not in any way a suitable husband, and her father had decided wisely. The poor girl lived in a constant atmosphere of petty persecution. Her father, she was told, might lose his post in the Bavarian service if she married this Socialist, her brother would have absolutely no career open to him, her sisters could not marry in their own rank of life; in fact, the whole family were alleged to be entirely unhappy and miserable through her stubbornness. The following letter—obviously dictated—was the not unnatural outcome:—

TO HERR LASSALLE.

SIR,—

I have again become reconciled to my betrothed bridegroom, Herr Yanko von Racowitza, whose love I have regained, and I deeply repent my earlier action. I have given notice of this to your legal representative, Herr Holthoff, and I now declare to you of my own free will and firm conviction, that there never can be any further question of a marriage between us, and that I hold myself in all respects to be released from such an engagement. I am now firmly resolved to devote to my aforesaid betrothed bridegroom my eternal love and fidelity.

HELENE VON DONNIGES.

This letter came through Rustow, and Lassalle addressed the following reply to Helen, which, however, she never received—it came in fact into the possession of the Countess—a sufficient commentary on the duplicity and the false friendship not only of Holthoff, but of Colonel Rustow and the Countess Hatzfeldt in this sad affair.

MUNICH, *Aug.* 20, 1864.

HELEN,—

My heart is breaking! Rustow's letter will kill me. That you have betrayed me seems impossible! Even now I cannot believe in such shamelessness, in such frightful treachery. It is only for a moment that some one has overridden your will and obliterated your true self. It is inconceivable that this can be your real, your abiding determination. You cannot have thrown aside all shame, all love, all fidelity, all truth. If you did, you would dishonour and disfigure humanity. There can be no truth left in the world if you are false, if you are capable of descending to this depth of abandonment, of breaking such holy oaths, of crushing my heart. Then there is nothing more under the sun in which a man can still believe.

Have you not filled me with a longing to possess you?

Have you not implored me to exhaust all proper measures, before carrying you away from Wabern? Have you not by your own lips and by your letters, sworn to me the most sacred oaths? Have you not declared to me, even in your last letters, that you were nothing, nothing but my loving wife, and that no power on earth should stay your resolution? And now, after you have bound this true heart of mine to yourself so strongly, this heart which when once it gives itself away gives itself for ever; now, when the battle has scarcely begun, do you cast me off? Do you betray me? Do you destroy me? If so, you succeed in doing what else no fate can do; you will have crushed and shattered one of the hardest of men, who could withstand unflinchingly all outward storms. No, I can never survive such treachery. It will kill me inwardly and outwardly. It is not possible that you are so dishonourable, so shameless, so reckless of duty, so utterly unworthy and infamous. If you were, you would deserve of me the most deadly hatred. You would deserve the contempt of the world. Helen, it is not your own resolution which you have communicated to Rustow. Some one has fastened it upon you by a coercion of your better feelings. Listen to me. If you abide by this resolution, you will lament it as long as you live.

Helen, true to my words, "*Je me charge du reste,*" I shall stay here, and shall take all possible steps to break down your father's opposition. I have already excellent means in my hand, which will certainly not remain unused, and if they do not succeed, I shall still possess thousands of other means, and I will grind all hindrances to dust if you will but remain true to me. If you remain true, there is no limit to my strength or to my love of you, *Je me charge toujours du reste!* The battle is hardly begun, you cowardly girl. But can it be, that while I sit here, and have already achieved what seemed impossible, you are betraying me, and listening to the flattering words of another man? Helen, my fate is in your hands! But if you destroy me by this wicked treachery, from which I cannot recover, then may evil fall upon you, and my curse follow you to the grave! This is the curse of a true heart, of a heart that you wantonly break, and with which you have cruelly trifled. Yes, this curse of mine will surely strike you.

According to Rustow's message, you want your letters to be returned to you. In any case, you will never receive them otherwise than from me—after a personal interview. For I must and will speak to you personally, and to you alone. I must and will hear my death-doom from your own lips. It is only thus that I can believe what otherwise seems impossible to me.

I am continuing here to take further steps to win you, and when I have done all that is possible, I shall come to Geneva. Helen, our destinies are entwined!

F. LASSALLE. {213}

It is pitiable to realize the amount of false or imperfect friendship which led Lassalle on to his ruin. Rustow was false, and Holthoff was false, if it were not rather that both looked upon Lassalle's affection for this girl, half his age, as a mad freak to be cured and forgotten. More might have been expected from the Countess, to whom Lassalle had given so much pure and disinterested devotion; but here again, a sense of maternal ownership in Lassalle was sufficient to justify, in such a woman, any means to keep him apart from this fancy of the hour. To the Countess, however, Helen had turned for help, and had received a note which had but enraged her, and made the breach between her and Lassalle yet wider. In the after years, Helen published one letter and the Countess another as the actual reply of the Countess to Helen's appeal, and the truth will now never be known. Meanwhile Dr. Arndt, a nephew of von Donniges, had gone to Berlin to fetch Yanko von Racowitza. Of Yanko Helen has herself given us a pleasant picture, as the one man for whom she really cared until the overwhelming presence of Lassalle appeared upon the scene, as her one friend during her persecution. Absent from Lassalle's influence, it was not strange that the delicate Wallachian—even younger than herself and the slave of her every whim—should have an influence in her life. Had Lassalle, however, had yet another personal interview with her, there can scarcely be a doubt that she would have been as he had once said, "as clay in the hands of the potter"—but this was not to be. Lassalle came back to Geneva on August 23, and immediately wrote an earnest letter to Herr von Donniges, begging for an interview, and stating that he had not the least enmity towards him for what had happened. With the fear of the Foreign Minister at Munich before his eyes Helen's father could not well refuse again, and the interview took place. Lassalle, according to von Donniges, demanded that Yanko von Racowitza should be forbidden the house, while he himself should have ready access to Helen. He further charged von Donniges with cruelty to his daughter, and was called a liar to his face, while even the cook was called upon the scene to give her evidence as to the domestic ethics of this family circle. The letter of von Donniges to Dr. Haenle was clearly meant to be shown to the Foreign Minister, and the wily diplomatist naturally took the opportunity both to justify himself and to vilify Lassalle. Then began a painful dispute as to whether Herr von Donniges had ill-used his daughter; the overwhelming evidence, which includes the testimony of that daughter, written long after her father's death, tending to prove the truth of Lassalle's allegation. Lassalle meanwhile found no opportunity of approaching Helen, and having every reason to believe that she was

Clement Shorter

entirely faithless, gave up the struggle. He referred to the girl in language characteristic of a despairing and jilted lover, and sent von Donniges a challenge, although many years before, in a political controversy, he had declined to fight—on principle. His seconds were to be General Becker and Colonel Rustow, and the latter has left us a long account of the affair.

On the appointed day, August 22, Rustow went everywhere to look for Herr von Donniges, but the minister had fled to Berne. Rustow then saw Lassalle at the rooms of the Countess von Hatzfeldt. Lassalle mentioned that he had that morning had his challenge accepted by von Racowitza, whose seconds were Count Keyserling and Dr. Arndt. Rustow insisted, both to Lassalle and to Racowitza's friends, that von Donniges should have priority, but was overruled; and it was agreed that the duel should be fought that very evening. Rustow protested that he could not find another second in so short a time—General Becker does not seem to have been available—but at length it was arranged that General Bethlem should be asked to fill the office, and that the duel should take place on the following morning, August 28. There seems to have been considerable difficulty in finding suitable pistols, and at the last moment General Bethlem declined to be a second, and Herr von Hofstetten consented to act. Rustow called upon Lassalle at the Victoria Hotel at five o'clock. At half-past six the party started for Carouge, a village in the neighbourhood of Geneva, which they reached an hour later. Lassalle was quite cheerful, and perfectly confident that he would come unharmed out of the conflict. The opponents faced one another and Racowitza wounded Lassalle, who was carried by Rustow and Dr. Seiler to a coach, and thence to the Victoria Hotel, Geneva. He suffered dreadfully both then and afterwards, and was only relieved by a plentiful use of opium. Three days later, on Wednesday, August 31, 1864, he died.

Was it the chance shot of a delicate boy that killed one of the most remarkable men of the nineteenth century, or was it a planned attack upon one who loved the people? This last view was taken and is still taken by many of his followers; but it is needless to say that it has no foundation in fact. Lassalle was killed by a chance shot, and killed in a duel which had not even the doubtful justification of hatred of his opponent. "Count me no longer as a rival; for you I have nothing but friendship," were the words written to Racowitza at the moment that he challenged von Donniges, and he declared on his death-bed that he died by his own hand.

The revolutionists of all lands assembled around his dead body, which was embalmed by order of the Countess. This woman talked loudly of vengeance, called not only von Racowitza but Helen a murderer, {218} little thinking that posterity would judge her more hardly than Helen. She proposed to take the corpse in solemn procession through Germany; but an order from the Prussian Government disturbed her plans, and at Breslau, Lassalle's native town, it was allowed to rest. Lassalle is buried in the family vault in the Jewish Cemetery, and a simple monument bears the inscription:

HERE RESTS WHAT IS MORTAL
OF
FERDINAND LASSALLE,
THE
THINKER AND THE FIGHTER.

To understand the whole tragedy and to justify its great victim is to feel something of the strain which comes to every thinker and fighter who, like Lassalle, writes and speaks persistently to vast audiences, often against great odds, and always with the prospect of a prison before him. That his nerves were utterly unstrung, that he was not his real self in those last days, is but too evident. Armed, as he claimed, with the entire culture of his century, a maker of history if ever there was one, he became the victim of a love drama which I suppose that Mr. Matthew Arnold would describe as of the surgeon's apprentice order: but which, apart from his political creed, will always endear him to men and women who have "lived and loved."

And what shall we say of Helen von Donniges? Her own story is surely one of the most romantic ever written. In *My Relation to Ferdinand Lassalle*, she tells how Yanko broke to her the news that he was going to fight Lassalle, and how much she grieved. "Lassalle will inevitably kill Yanko," she thought; and she pitied him, but her pity was not without calculation. "When Yanko is dead and they bring his body here, there will be a stir in the house," she said, "and I can then fly to Lassalle." But the hours flew by, and finally Yanko came to tell her that he had wounded his opponent. For the moment, and indeed until after Lassalle's death, she hated her successful lover; but a little later his undoubted goodness, his tenderness and patience, won her heart. They were married, but he died within a year, of consumption. Being disowned by her relations, Helen then settled in Berlin, and studied for the stage. She herself relates how at Breslau on one occasion, when acting a boy's part in one of Moser's comedies, some of Lassalle's oldest friends being present remarked upon her likeness to Lassalle in his youth, a resemblance on which she and Lassalle had more than once prided themselves. At a later date Frau von Racowitza married a Russian Socialist, S. E. Shevitch, then resident in America. M. Shevitch returned to Russia a few years after this and lived with his wife at Riga. Those who have seen Madame Shevitch describe her as one of the most fascinating women they have ever met. She and her husband were very happy in their married life. Madame Shevitch is now living in Munich. Our great novelist and poet George Meredith has immortalized her in his *Tragic Comedians*.

VIII

LORD ACTON'S LIST OF
THE HUNDRED BEST BOOKS

Every one has heard of Lord Avebury's (Sir John Lubbock's) Hundred Best Books, not every one of Lord Acton's. It is the privilege of the *Pall Mall Magazine* {225} to publish this latter list, the final impression as to reading of one of the most scholarly men that England has known in our time. The list in question is, as it were, an omitted chapter of a book that was one of the successes of its year—*The Letters of Lord Acton to Miss Mary Gladstone*—published by Mr. George Allen. That series of letters made very pleasant reading. They showed Lord Acton not as a Dryasdust, but as a very human personage indeed, with sympathies invariably in the right place.

Nor can his literary interests be said to have been restricted, for he read history and biography with avidity, and probably knew more of theology than any other layman of modern times. In imaginative literature, however, his critical instinct was perhaps less keen. He called Heine "a bad second to Schiller in poetry," which is absurd; and he thought George Eliot the greatest of modern novelists. In arriving at the latter judgment he had the excuse of personal friendship and admiration for a woman whose splendid intellectual gifts were undeniable.

In one letter we find Lord Acton discussing with Miss Gladstone the eternal question of the hundred best books. Sir John Lubbock had complained to her of the lack of a guide or supreme authority on the choice of books. Lord Acton had replied that, "although he had something to learn on the graver side of human knowledge," Sir John would execute his own scheme better than almost anybody. We all know that Sir John Lubbock attempted this at a lecture delivered at the Great Ormond Street Working Men's College; that that lecture has been reprinted again and again in a book entitled *The Pleasures of Life*, and that the publishers have sold more than two hundred thousand copies—a kind of success that might almost make some of our popular novelists turn green with envy. Later on in the correspondence Lord Acton quoted one of the popes, who said that "fifty books would include every good idea in the world." "But," continued Lord Acton, "literature has doubled since then, and it would be hard to do without a hundred."

Lord Acton was possessed of the happy thought that he would like some of his friends and acquaintances each to name his ideal hundred best books—as for example Bishop Lightfoot, Dean Church, Dean Stanley, Canon Liddon, Professor Max Muller, Mr. J. R. Lowell, Professor E. A. Freeman, Mr. W. E. H. Lecky, Mr. John Morley, Sir Henry Maine, the Duke of Argyll, Lord Tennyson, Cardinal Newman, Mr. Gladstone, Matthew Arnold, Professor Goldwin Smith, Mr. R. H. Hutton, Mr. Mark Pattison, and Mr. J. A. Symonds. Strange to say, he thought there would be a surprising agreement between these writers as to which were the hundred best books. I am all but certain, however, that there would not have been more than twenty books in common between rival schools of thought—the secular and the ecclesiastical—between, let us say, Mr. John Morley and

Cardinal Newman. But it is probable that not one of these eminent men would have furnished a list with any similarity whatever to the remainder. Each would have written down his own hundred favourites, and herein may be admitted is an evidence of the futility of all such attempts. The best books are the books that have helped us most to see life in all its complex bearings, and each individual needs a particular kind of mental food quite unlike the diet that best stimulates his neighbour. Writing more than a year later, Lord Acton said that he had just drawn out a list of recommended authors for his son, as being the company he would like him to keep; but this list is not available—it is not the one before me. That was compiled yet another twelve months afterwards, when we find Lord Acton sending to Miss Mary Gladstone (Mrs. Drew) his own ideal "hundred best books." This list is now printed for the first time. Evidently Miss Gladstone remonstrated with her friend over the character of the list; but Lord Acton defended it as being in his judgment really the hundred *best books*, apart from works on physical science—that it treated of principles that every thoughtful man ought to understand, and was calculated, in fact, to give one a clear view of the various forces that make history. "We are not considering," he adds, "what will suit an untutored savage or an illiterate peasant woman, who would never come to an end of the *Imitation*."

However, here is Lord Acton's list, which Mrs. Drew has been kind enough to place in the hands of the Editor of the *Pall Mall Magazine*. I give also Lord Acton's comment with which it opens, and I add in footnotes one or two facts about each of the authors:

* * * * *

"In answer to the question: Which are the hundred best books in the world?

"Supposing any English youth, whose education is finished, who knows common things, and is not training for a profession.

"To perfect his mind and open windows in every direction, to raise him to the level of his age so that he may know the (20 or 30) forces that have made our world what it is and still reign over it, to guard him against surprises and against the constant sources of error within, to supply him both with the strongest stimulants and the surest guides, to give force and fullness and clearness and sincerity and independence and elevation and generosity and serenity to his mind, that he may know the method and law of the process by which error is conquered and truth is won, discerning knowledge from probability and prejudice from belief, that he may learn to master what he rejects as fully as what he adopts, that he may understand the origin as well as the strength and vitality of systems and the better motive of men who are wrong, to steel him against the charm of literary beauty and talent; so that each book, thoroughly taken in, shall be the beginning of a new life, and shall make a new man of him—this list is submitted":—

1. Plato—*Laws*—Steinhart's *Introduction*. {230a}

2. Aristotle—*Politics*—Susemihl's *Commentary*. {230b}

3. Epictetus—*Encheiridion*—*Commentary* of Simplicius. {230c}

4. St. Augustine—*Letters*. {230d}

5. St. Vincent's *Commonitorium*. {231a}

6. Hugo of S. Victor—*De Sacramentis*. {231b}

7. St. Bonaventura—*Breviloquium.* {231c}

8. St. Thomas Aquinas—*Summa contra Gentiles.* {231d}

9. Dante—*Divina Commedia.* {232a}

10. Raymund of Sabunde—*Theologia Naturalis.* {232b}

11. Nicholas of Cusa—*Concordantia Catholica.* {232c}

12. Edward Reuss—*The Bible.* {232d}

13. Pascal's Pensees—*Havet's Edition.* {233a}

14. Malebranche, *De la Recherche de la Verite.* {233b}

15. Baader—*Speculative Dogmatik.* {233c}

16. Molitor—*Philosophie der Geschichte.* {233d}

17. Astie—*Esprit de Vinet.* {233e}

18. Punjer—*Geschichte der Religions-philosophie.* {234a}

19. Rothe—*Theologische Ethik.* {234b}

20. Martensen—*Die Christliche Ethik.* {234c}

21. Oettingen—*Moralstatistik.* {234d}

22. Hartmann—*Phanomenologie des sittlichen Bewusstseins.* {234e}

23. Leibniz—*Letters* edited by Klopp. {235a}

24. Brandis—*Geschichte der Philosophie.* {235b}

25. Fischer—*Franz Bacon*. {235c}

26. Zeller—*Neuere Deutsche Philosophie*. {235d}

27. Bartholomess—*Doctrines Religieuses de la Philosophie Moderns*. {236a}

28. Guyon—*Morale Anglaise*. {236b}

29. Ritschl—*Entstehung der Altkatholischen Kirche*. {236c}

30. Loening—*Geschichte des Kirchenrechts*. {236d}

31. Baur—*Vorlesungen uber Dogmengeschichte*. {237a}

32. Fenelon—*Correspondence*. {237b}

33. Newman's *Theory of Development*. {237c}

34. Mozley's *University Sermons*. {237d}

35. Schneckenburger—*Vergleichende Darstellung*. {238a}

36. Hundeshagen—*Kirckenvorfassungsgeschichte*. {238b}

37. Schweizer—*Protestantische Centraldogmen*. {238c}

38. Gass—*Geschichte der Lutherischen Dogmatik*. {238d}

39. Cart—*Histoire du Mouvement Religieux dans le Canton de Vaud*. {238e}

40. Blondel—*De la Primaute*. {239a}

41. Le Blanc de Beaulieu—*Theses*. {239b}

42. Thiersch.—*Vorlesungen uber Katholizismus*. {239c}

43. Mohler—*Neue Untersuchungen*. {239d}

44. Scherer—*Melanges de Critique Religieuse*. {240a}

45. Hooker—*Ecclesiastical Polity*. {240b}

46. Weingarten—*Revolutionskirchen Englands*. {240c}

47. Kliefoth—*Acht Bucher von der Kirche*. {240d}

48. Laurent—*Etudes de l'Histoire de l'Humanite*. {240e}

49. Ferrari—*Revolutions de l'Italie*. {241a}

50. Lange—*Geschichte des Materialismus*. {241b}

51. Guicciardini—*Ricordi Politici*. {241c}

52. Duperron—*Ambassades*. {241d}

53. Richelieu—*Testament Politique*. {242a}

54. Harrington's Writings. {242b}

55. Mignet—*Negotiations de la Succession d'Espagne*. {242c}

56. Rousseau—*Considerations sur la Pologne*. {243a}

57. Foncin—*Ministere de Turgot*. {243b}

58. Burke's *Correspondence*. {243c}

59. Las Cases—*Memorial de Ste. Helene*. {243d}

60. Holtzendorff—*Systematische Rechtsenzyklopadie.* {244a}

61. Jhering—*Geist des Romischen Rechts.* {244b}

62. Geib—*Strafrecht.* {244c}

63. Maine—*Ancient Law.* {245a}

64. Gierke—*Genossenschaftsrecht.* {245b}

65. Stahl—*Philosophie des Rechts.* {245c}

66. Gentz—*Briefwechsel mit Adam Muller.* {246a}

67. Vollgraff—*Polignosie.* {246b}

68. Frantz—*Kritik aller Parteien.* {246c}

69. De Maistre—*Considerations sur la France.* {246d}

70. Donoso Cortes—*Ecrits Politiques.* {247a}

71. Perin—*De la Richesse dans les Societes Chretiennes.* {247b}

72. Le Play—*La Reforme Sociale.* {247c}

73. Riehl—*Die Burgerliche Sociale.* {247d}

74. Sismondi—*Etudes sur les Constitutions des Peuples Libres.* {248a}

75. Rossi—*Cours du Droit Constitutionnel.* {248b}

76. Barante—*Vie de Royer Collard.* {248c}

77. Duvergier de Hauranne—*Histoire du Gouvernement Parlementaire.* {249a}

78. Madison—*Debates of the Congress of Confederation.* {249b}

79. Hamilton—*The Federalist.* {249c}

80. Calhoun—*Essay on Government.* {249d}

81. Dumont—*Sophismes Anarchiques.* {250a}

82. Quinet—*La Revolution Francaise.* {250b}

83. Stein—*Sozialismus in Frankreich.* {250c}

84. Lassalle—*System der Erworbenen Rechte.* {251a}

85. Thonissen—*Le Socialisme depuis l'Antiquite.* {251b}

86. Considerant—*Destines Sociale.* {251c}

87. Roscher—*Nationalokonomik.* {251d}

89. Mill—*System of Logic.* {251e}

90. Coleridge—*Aids to Reflection.* {252a}

91. Radowitz—*Fragmente.* {252b}

92. Gioberti—*Pensieri.* {252c}

93. Humboldt—*Kosmos.* {253a}

94. De Candolle—*Histoire des Sciences et des Savants.* {253b}

95. Darwin—*Origin of Species*. {253c}

96. Littre—*Fragments de Philosophie*. {253d}

97. Cournot—*Enchainements des Idees fondamentales*. {253e}

98. *Monatschriften der wissenschaftlichen Vereine*. {254}

This list, written in 1883 in Miss Gladstone's (Mrs. Drew's) Diary, must always have an interest in the history of the human mind.

But my readers will, I imagine, for the most part, agree with me that there are others besides untutored savages and illiterate peasant women to whom such a list is entirely impracticable. It indicates the enormous preference which on the whole Lord Acton gave to the Literature of Knowledge over the Literature of Power, to use De Quincey's famous distinction. With the exception of Dante's *Divine Comedy* there is practically not a single book that has any title whatever to a place in the Literature of Power, a literature which many of us think the only thing in the world of books worth consideration. Great philosophy is here, and high thought. Who would for a moment wish to disparage St. Bonaventure, the Seraphic Doctor, or Aquinas the Angelic? Plato and Pascal, Malebranche and Fenelon, Bossuet and Machiavelli are all among the world's immortals. Yet now and again we are bewildered by finding the least important book of a well-known author—as for example Rousseau's *Poland* instead of the *Confessions* and Coleridge's *Aids to Reflection* instead of the *Poems* or the *Biographia Literaria*. Think of an historian whose ideal of historical work was so high that he despised all who worked only from printed documents, selecting the *Memorial of St. Helena* of Las Casas in preference not only to a hundred- and-one similar compilations concerning Napoleon's exile, but in preference to Thucydides, Herodotus and Gibbon.

Sometimes Lord Acton names a theologian who is absolutely out-of-date, at others a philosopher who is in the same case. But on the whole it is a fascinating list as an index to what a well-trained mind thought the noblest mental equipment for life's work. At the best, it is true, it would represent but one half of life. But then Lord Acton recognized this when he asked that men should be "steeled against the charm of literary beauty and talent," and he was assuming in any case that all the books in aesthetic literature, the best poetry and the best history had already been read, as he undoubtedly had read them.

"The charm of literary beauty and talent!" There is the whole question. Nothing really matters for the average man, so far as books are concerned, but this charm, and I am criticizing Lord Acton's list for the average man. The student who has got beyond it need not worry himself about classified lists. He may read his Plato, and Aristotle, his Pascal and Newman, his Christian apologists and German theologians, as he wills; or he may read in some other quite different direction. Guidance is impossible to a mind at such a stage of cultivation as Lord Acton had in view.

Only minds at a more primitive stage of culture than this most learned and most accomplished man seemed able to conceive of, could be bettered by advice as to reading. Given, indeed, contact with some superior mind, which out of its rich equipment of culture should advise as to the books that might be most profitably read, I could imagine advice being helpful. It would be of no value, it is true, to an untutored savage or illiterate peasant, but to a youth fresh from school-books and much modern fiction, to a young girl about to enter upon life in its more serious aspects, it would be immensely serviceable. It was of such as these that Mr. Ruskin thought when he wrote of "King's Treasures" in *Sesame and Lilies*, and the same idea was doubtless in Sir John Lubbock's mind when he lectured on the "Hundred Best Books." But Lord Avebury's list had its limitations, it seems to me, for any one who has an interest in good literature and guidance to the reading thereof. To give "Scott" as one book and "Shakspere" as another was I suggest to shirk much responsibility of selection. Scott is a whole library, Shakspere is yet another. One may give "Keats" or "Shelley" because they are more limited in quantity. Even to name novels by Charles Kingsley and Bulwer Lytton in this select hundred was to demonstrate to men of this generation that Lord Avebury being of an earlier one had a bias in favour of the books that we are all outgrowing. To include Mill's *Logic* is to ignore the Time Spirit acting on philosophy; to include Tennyson's *Idylls* its action on poetry. Mill and Tennyson will always live in literature but not I think by these books.

But the fact is that there is no possibility of naming the hundred best books. No one could quarrel with Lord Avebury if he had named these as his hundred own favourites among the books of the world. Still, it might have been *his* hundred; it could not possibly have been any one else's hundred because every man of education must make his own choice. No! the naming of the hundred best books for any large, general audience is quite impossible. All that is possible in such a connexion is to state emphatically that there are very few books that are equally suitable to every kind of intellect. Temperament as well as intellectual endowment make for so much in reading. Take, for example, the *Imitation* of *Christ*. George Eliot, although not a Christian, found it soul-satisfying. Thackeray, as I think a more robust intellect, found it well nigh as mischievous as did Eugene Sue, whose anathematizations in his novel *The Wandering Jew* are remembered by all. Other books that have been the outcome of piety of mind leave less room for difference of opinion. Surely Dante's *Divine Comedy*, and Bunyan's *Pilgrim's Progress*, make an universal appeal. That universal appeal is the point at which alone guidance is possible. There are great books that can be read only by the few, but surely the very greatest appeal alike to the educated and the illiterate, to the man of rich intellectual endowment and to the man to whom all processes of reasoning are incomprehensible. *Hamlet* is a wonderful test of this quality. It "holds the boards" at the small provincial theatre, it is enacted by Mr. Crummles to an illiterate peasantry, and it is performed by the greatest actor to the most select city audience. It is made the subject of study by learned commentators. It is world-embracing.

Are there in the English language, including translations, a hundred books that stand the test as *Hamlet* stands it? No two men would make the same list of books that answer to this demand of an universal appeal, and obviously each nation must make its own list. Mine is for English boys and girls just growing into manhood and womanhood, or for those who have had no educational advantages in early years. I exclude living writers, and I give the hundred in four groups.

POETRY.

1. The Bible. {260a}

2. *The Odyssey*, translated by Butcher and Lang. {260b}

3. The *Iliad*, translated by Lang, Leaf and Myers. {260b}

4. Aeschylus, translated by George Warr. {261a}

5. Sophocles, translated by J. S. Phillimore. {261a}

6. Euripides, translated by Gilbert Murray. {261a}

7. Virgil, translated by Dryden. {261b}

8. Catullus, translated by Theodore Martin. {261c}

9. Horace, translated by Theodore Martin. {261d}

10. Dante, translated by Cary. {262a}

11. Shakspere, *Hamlet*. {262b}

12. Chaucer, *Canterbury Tales*. {262c}

13. FitzGerald, *Omar Khayyam*. {263a}

14. Goethe, *Faust*. {263b}

15. Shelley. {263c}

16. Byron. {263d}

17. Wordsworth. {264a}

18. Keats. {264b}

19. Burns. {264c}

20. Coleridge. {264d}

21. Cowper. {264e}

22. Crabbe. {265a}

23. Tennyson. {265b}

24. Browning. {265c}

25. Milton. {265d}

FICTION.

1. *The Arabian Nights Entertainment.* {266a}

2. *Don Quixote*, by Cervantes. {266b}

3. *Pilgrim's Progress*, by Bunyan. {266c}

4. *Robinson Crusoe*, by Defoe. {266d}

5. *Gulliver's Travels*, by Swift. {267a}

6. *Clarissa*, by Richardson. {267b}

7. *Tom Jones*, by Fielding. {267c}

8. *Rasselas*, by Johnson. {267d}

9. *Vicar of Wakefield*, by Goldsmith. {268a}

10. *Sentimental Journey*, by Sterne. {268b}

11. *Nightmare Abbey*, by Peacock. {268c}

12. *Kenilworth*, by Walter Scott. {268d}

13. *Pere Goriot*, by Balzac. {268e}

14. *The Three Musketeers*, by Dumas. {269a}

15. *Vanity Fair*, by Thackeray. {269b}

16. *Villette*, by Charlotte Bronte. {269c}

17. *David Copperfield*, by Charles Dickens. {269d}

18. *Barchester Towers*, by Anthony Trollope. {269e}

19. Boccaccio's *Decameron*. {269f}

20. *Wuthering Heights*, by Emily Bronte. {270a}

21. *The Cloister and the Hearth*, by Charles Reade. {270b}

22. *Les Miserables*, by Victor Hugo. {270c}

23. *Cranford*, by Mrs. Gaskell. {270d}

24. *Consuelo*, by George Sand. {270e}

25. *Charles O'Malley*, by Charles Lever. {270f}

MISCELLANEOUS
HISTORY, ESSAYS, ETC

1. Macaulay, *History of England*. {271a}

2. Carlyle, *Past and Present*. {271b}

3. Motley, *Dutch Republic*. {271c}

4. Gibbon, *Decline and Fall of the Roman Empire*. {271d}

5. Plutarch's *Lives*. {272a}

6. Montaigne's *Essays*. {272b}

7. Richard Steele, *Essays*. {272c}

8. Lamb, *Essays of Elia*. {272d}

9. De Quincey, *Opium Eater*. {272e}

10. Hazlitt, *Essays*. {273a}

11. Borrow, *Lavengro*. {273b}

12. Emerson, *Representative Men*. {273c}

13. Landor, *Imaginary Conversations*. {273d}

14. Arnold, *Essays in Criticism*. {273e}

15. Herodotus, *Macaulay's Translation*. {273f}

16. Howell's *Familiar Letters*. {274a}

17. Buckle's *History of Civilization*. {274b}

18. Tacitus, Church and Brodribb's Translation. {274c}

19. Mitford's *Our Village*. {274d}

20. Green's *Short History of the English People*. {274e}

21. Taine, *Ancient Regime*. {275a}

22. Bourrienne, *Napoleon*. {275b}

23. Tocqueville, *Democracy in America.* {275c}

24. Walton, *Compleat Angler.* {275d}

25 White, *Natural History of Selbourne.* {276a}

BIOGRAPHICAL AND AUTOBIOGRAPHICAL

1. Boswell's Johnson. {276b}

2. Lockhart's Scott. {276c}

3. Pepys's Diary. {276d}

4. Walpole's Letters. {277a}

5. The Memoirs of Count de Gramont. {277b}

6. Gray's Letters. {277c}

7. Southey's Nelson. {277d}

8. Moore's Byron. {277e}

9. Hogg's Shelley. {278a}

10. Rousseau's Confessions. {278b}

11. Froude's Carlyle. {278c}

12. Rogers's Table Talk. {279a}

13. Confessions of St. Augustine. {279b}

14. Amiel's Journal. {279c}

15. Meditations of Marcus Aurelius. {279d}

16. Lewes's Life of Goethe. {279e}

17. Sime's Life of Lessing. {280a}

18. Franklin's Autobiography. {280b}

19. Greville's Memoirs. {280c}

20. Forster's Life of Dickens. {280d}

21. Madame D'Arblay's Diary. {280e}

22. Newman's Apologia. {281a}

23. The Paston Letters. {281b}

24. Cellini's Autobiography. {281c}

25. Browne's Religio Medici. {281d}

My readers for the most part have read every one of these books. I throw out this list as a tentative effort in the direction of suggesting a hundred books with which to start a library. The young student will find much to amuse, and certainly nothing here to bore him. These books will not make him a prig, as Mr. James Payn said that Lord Avebury's list would make him a prig. They will make the dull man less dull, the bright man brighter. Here is good, cheerful, robust reading for boy and girl, for man and woman. There are many sins of omission, but none of commission. Our young friend will add to this list fast enough, but there is nothing in it that he may not read with profit. These books, I repeat, make an universal appeal. The learned man may enjoy them, the unlearned may enjoy them also. They are, as *Hamlet* is, of universal interest. Devotion to science will not impair a taste for them, nor will zest for abstract speculations. Not even those who are "better skilled in grammar than in poetry" can fail to appreciate. These hundred books will in the main be the hundred best books of many of my readers who are quite capable of selecting for themselves. One last word of advice. Let not the young reader buy large quantities of books at once or be beguiled into subscribing for some cheap series which will save him the trouble of selecting. He may buy many books from such cheap series afterwards, but not his first hundred, I think. These should be acquired through much saving, and purchased with great thought and deliberation. The purchase of a book should become to the young book-lover a most solemn function.

Butler and Tanner, The Selwood Printing Works, Frome, and London

Footnotes:

{3} Richard Garnett (1835-1906) was son of the philologist of the same name who was for a time priest-vicar of Lichfield Cathedral. He attended the Johnson Celebration on Sept. 18, 1905, and proposed "the Immortal Memory of Dr. Johnson." He died on the following Good Friday, April 13, and was buried in Highgate Cemetery April 17, 1906.

{6} Anna Seward (1747-1809). Her works were published after her death:—*The Poetical Works of Anna Seward. With Extracts from her Literary Correspondence.* Edited by Walter Scott, Esq. In three volumes—*John Ballantyne &*

Co., 1810. *Letters of Anna Seward written between the Years* 1784 *and* 1807. In six volumes. Archibald Constable & Co., 1811. "Longwinded and florid" one biographer calls her letters, but by the aid of what Scott calls 'the laudable practice of skipping' they are quite entertaining.

{8} Sir Robert Thomas White-Thomson, K.C.B., wrote to me in reference to this estimate of Miss Seward from Broomford Manor, Exbourne, North Devon, and his letter seemed of sufficient importance from a genealogical standpoint for me to ask his permission to make an extract from the letter: "I have read your address in a Lichfield newspaper. Apart from the wider and more important bearings of your words, those which had reference to the Seward family were especially welcome to me. You will understand this when I tell you that, with the exception of the Romney portrait of Anna, and a few other objects left 'away' by her will, my grandfather, Thomas White, of Lichfield Close, her cousin and residuary legatee, became possessed of all the contents of her house. Some of the books and engravings were sold by auction, but the remainder were taken good care of, and passed to me on my mother's death in 1860. As thus, 'in a way' the representative of the 'Swan of Lichfield,' you can easily see what such an appreciation of her as was yours means to me. Of course I know her weak points, and how the pot of clay must suffer in trying to 'bump' the pot of iron in midstream, but I also know that she was no ordinary personage in her day, when the standard of feminine culture was low, and I have resented some things that have been written of her. Mrs. Oliphant treats her kindly in her *Literary History of England*, and now I have your 'appreciation' of her, for which I beg to thank you."

{15} Once certainly in the lines "On the Death of Mr. Robert Levet":—

Well try'd through many a varying year,
See Levet to the grave descend,
Officious, innocent, sincere,
Of ev'ry friendless name the friend.

{18} *Prayers and Meditations*: composed by Samuel Johnson, LL.D., and published from his Manuscripts by George Straham, D.D., Prebendary of Rochester and Vicar of Islington in Middlesex, 1785. Dr. Birkbeck Hill suggests that Johnson could not have contemplated the publication of the work in its entirety, but the world is the better for the self revelation, notwithstanding Cowper's remark in a letter to Newton (August 27, 1785), that "the publisher of it is neither much a friend to the cause of religion nor to the author's memory; for by the specimen of it that has reached us, it seems to contain only such stuff as has a direct tendency to expose both to ridicule."

{19} There is an edition with a brief Introduction by Augustine Birrell, published by Elliot Stock in 1904, and another, with an Introduction by "H. C.," was issued by H. R. Allenson in 1906.

{31} The Rev. Angus Mackay, author of *The Brontes In Fact and Fiction*. He was Rector of Holy Trinity Church, Dean Bridge, Edinburgh, when he died, aged 54, on New Year's Day, 1907. Earlier in life he had been a Curate at Olney.

{34} John Newton (1725-1807) had been the captain of a slave ship before his 'conversion.' He became Curate of Olney in 1764 and published the famous Olney Hymns with Cowper in 1779. In 1780 Newton became the popular Incumbent of St. Mary Woolnoth, London.

{35} See the Globe *Cowper*, with an Introduction by the

Rev. William Benham, the Rector of St. Edmund's, Lombard Street. Canon Benham has written many books, but he has done no better piece of work than this fine Introduction which first appeared in 1870.

{36} Thomas Scott (1747-1821). His commentaries first appeared in weekly parts between 1788 and 1792, and were first issued in ten volumes, 1823-25. He was Rector of Astin Sandford in Buckinghamshire from 1801 until his death. His *Life* was published by his son, the Rev. John Scott, in 1822.

{37} Thomas Percy (1729-1811) became Vicar of Easton Maudit, Northamptonshire, in 1753. Johnson visited him here in 1764. In 1765 Percy published his *Reliques of Ancient English Poetry*. He became Bishop of Dromere in 1782.

{38a} William Hayley (1745-1820) was counted a great poet in his day and placed in the same rank with Dryden and Pope. He wrote *Triumphs of Temper* 1781, *Triumphs of Music* 1804, and many other works; but he is of interest here by virtue of his *Life and Letters of William Cowper, Esq., with Remarks on Epistolary Writers*, published in 1803.

{38b} Robert Southey (1774-1843), whose *Life and Works of Cowper* is in fifteen volumes, which were published by Baldwin & Cradock between the years 1835 and 1837. The attractive form in which the works are presented, the many fine steel engravings, and the excellent type make this still the only way for book lovers to approach Cowper. Southey had to suffer the competition of the Rev. T. S. Grimshawe, who produced, through Saunders & Otley, about the same time a reprint of Hayley's biography with much of Cowper's correspondence that is not in Southey's volumes. The whole correspondence was collected by Mr. Thomas Wright, and published by Hodder & Stoughton in 1904.

{38c} Walter Bagehot (1826-1877) in his *Literary Studies*. James Russell Lowell (1819-1891) in his *Essays*. Mrs. Oliphant (1828-1897) in her *Literary History of England*; and George Eliot (1819-1880) in her *Essays* (Worldliness and Other Worldliness).

{44} It has no bearing upon the subject that the horrors of the Bastille at the time of its fall were greatly exaggerated.

{47} *Theology in the English Poets*, by Stopford A. Brooke.

{56} Mr. Leslie Stephen, who became Sir Leslie Stephen, K.C.B., in 1902, was born in 1832 and died in 1904. In addition to the article in the *D.N.B.*, this great critic has one on "Cowper and Rousseau" in his *Hours in a Library*.

{62} Sir John Fenn (1739-1794), the antiquary, obtained the originals of the *Paston Letters* from Thomas Worth, a chemist of Diss. The following lines were first printed in Cowper's Collected Poems, by Mr. J. C. Bailey in his admirable edition of 1906, published by the Methuens:—

Two omens seem propitious to my fame,
Your spouse embalms my verse, and you my name;
A name, which, all self-flattery far apart
Belongs to one who venerates in his heart
The wise and good, and therefore of the few
Known by these titles, sir, both yours and you.

They were written to please his cousin John Johnson who was to oblige Fenn by giving him an autograph of Cowper's.

{66} Edward Stanley (1779-1849), the father of Arthur Penrhyn Stanley (1815-1881), Dean of Westminster, was Bishop of Norwich from 1837 to 1849.

{80} Borrow's step-daughter, Henrietta Clarke, married James McOubrey, an Irish doctor. She outlived Borrow for many years, dying at Great Yarmouth in 1904. All her literary effects, including many interesting manuscripts, have been passed on to me by her executor, Mr. Hubert Smith, and these will be used in my forthcoming biography of Borrow.

{84} I ventured to ask my friend Mr. Birrell for a line to read to my Norwich audience and he sent me the following characteristic letter dated December 8, 1903:—

". . . For my part I should leave George Borrow alone, to take his own part even as Isopel Berners learnt to take hers in the great house at Long Melford. He has an appealing voice which no sooner falls on the ear of the born Borrovian, than up the lucky fellow must get and follow his master to the end of the chapter.

"However, if you will insist upon going out into the highways and hedges and compelling the wayfaring man— though a fool—to come in and take a seat at the *Lavengro* feast, nobody can stop you."

"The great thing is to get people to read the Borrow books: there is nothing else to be done. If, after having read them, some enthusiasts go on to learn *Romany* and seek to trace authorities on Gypsies and Gypsy lore—why, let them. They may soon know more about Gypsies than Borrow ever did— but they will never write about them as he did.

"The essence of the matter is to enjoy Borrow's books for themselves alone. As for Borrow's biography, it appears to me either that he has already written it, or it is not worth writing. Anyhow, place the books in the forefront, reprint things as often as you dare without *note or comment* or even *prefatory appreciation*, and you cannot but earn the gratitude of every true Borrovian who in consequence of your efforts come upon the Borrow books for the first time."

{97} M. Rene Huchon, who addressed the visitors at the Crabbe Celebration, published his *George Crabbe and his Times: A Critical and Biographical Study*, through Mr. John Murray, early in the present year, 1907.

{98} This reproach has since been removed by the appearance of the *Complete Works of George Crabbe* in three volumes of the Cambridge English Classics Series, published by the Cambridge University Press, and edited by Dr. A. W. Ward, the Master of Peterhouse.

{100} The original letter is in the possession of Mr. A. M. Broadley, of Bridport. It is reprinted from the Hanmer Correspondence in an appendix to M. Huchon's biography.

{106} But M. Huchon makes it clear in *George Crabbe and his Times* that Crabbe declined at the last moment to marry Miss Charlotte Ridout, who seems to have been really in love with him.

{138} This monument, a fine statue facing the house which replaces the one in which Sir Thomas Browne lived, was unveiled in October, 1905.

{144} For every student Cunningham's nine volumes have been superseded since this Address was delivered by the sixteen volumes of the Letters of Horace Walpole, edited by Mrs. Paget Toynbee for the Clarendon Press.

{145} The other side of the picture may, however, be presented. Horace, says Cunningham (Walpole's *Letters*, vol. i.), hated Norfolk, the native country of his father, and delighted in Kent, the native country of his mother. "He did not care for Norfolk ale, Norfolk turnips, Norfolk dumplings and Norfolk turkeys. Its flat, sandy aguish scenery was not to his taste." He dearly liked what he calls most happily, "the rich, blue prospects of Kent."

{153} Goldsmith doubtless had more than one experience in his mind when he wrote of:—

Sweet Auburn! loveliest village of the plain.

Lissoy, near Ballymahon, Ireland, served to provide many concrete features of the picture, but that the author drew upon his experiences of Houghton is believed by his principal biographer, John Forster, by Professor Masson and others, and on no other assumption than that of an English village can the lines be explained:—

A time there was, ere England's griefs began,
When every rood of ground maintained its man.

{185} Originally written to serve as an Introduction to an edition of Mr. George Meredith's *Tragic Comedians*, of which book Lassalle is the hero. That edition was published by Messrs. Ward Lock & Bowden, who afterwards transferred all rights in it to Messrs. Archibald Constable & Co., by whose courtesy the paper is included here.

{186} Lassalle's *Tagebuch*, edited by Paul Lindau, 1891.

{187} *Henrich Heine's sammtliche Werke*, vol. xxii., pp. 84-99.

{188} The most concise account of the affair is contained in the story of Sophie Solutzeff, entitled, *Eine Liebes-episode aus dem Leben Ferdinand Lassalle's*. This booklet, which is published in German, French, and Russian, professes to be an account of Lassalle's love for a young Russian lady, Sophie Solutzeff, some two years before he met Helene von Donniges. He is represented as being himself in a frenzy of passion; the lady, however, rejecting as a lover the man she had been prepared to worship as a teacher. There can be little doubt that the whole story is a fabrication, in which the Countess von Hatzfeldt had a considerable part. The Countess was rightly judged by popular opinion to have played a discreditable role in the love passages between Lassalle and Helene; and Helene's own account of the matter in her *Reminiscences* was an additional blow at the pseudo-friend who might have helped the lovers so much. What more natural than that the Countess should be anxious to break the force of Helene's indictment, by endorsing the popular, and indeed accurate judgment, that Lassalle was very inflammable where women were concerned. This she could do by depicting him, a little earlier, in precisely similar bondage to that which he had professed to Helene. That the Countess wrote, or assisted to write, the compilation of letters and diaries, does not, however, destroy its value as a record of Lassalle's struggle on her behalf. That account, if not written by Lassalle, was written or inspired by the other great actor in the Hatzfeldt drama, and may therefore be considered a fairly safe guide in recounting the story. Mr. Israel Zangwill, since the above was written, has published an article on Lassalle in his *Dreamers of the Ghetto*. He accepts Sophie Solutzeff's story as genuine, but that is merely the credulity of an accomplished romancer.

{198} Debate in the German Reichstag, April 2, 1881. Quoted by W. H. Dawson.

{213} Becker's *Enthullungen*, 1868.

{218} Briefe an Hans von Bulow, 1885.

{225} Reprinted with alterations from the *Pall Mall Magazine* of July, 1905, by kind permission of the proprietor and editor; and of Miss Mary Gladstone (Mrs. Drew) to whom the list of books was sent in a letter.

{230a} Plato (B.C. 427-347). Dr. Jowett has translated the *Laws*. See *The Dialogues* of Plato With Analysis and Introductions by Benjamin Jowett. In Five Volumes. Vol. V. The Clarendon Press.

{230b} Aristotle (B.C. 384-322). Dr. Jowett has translated the *Politics* into English. Two volumes. The Clarendon Press.

{230c} Epictetus (born A.D. 50, died in Rome, but date unknown). His *Encheiridion*, a collection of Maxims, was made by his pupil Arrian. The best translation into English is that by George Long, first published in 1877. (George Bell.)

{230d} St. Augustine (A.D. 353-430). See a translation of his *Letters* edited by Mary Allies, published in 1890.

{231a} St. Vincent of Lerins—Vincentius Lirinensis. Native of Gaul. Monk in monastery of Lerinat, opposite Cannes. Died about 450. In 434 wrote *Commonitorium adversus profanus omnium heretiecrum novitates*. It contains the famous threefold text of orthodoxy—"quod ubique, quod semper, quod ad omnibus creditum est." Printed at Paris, 1663 and later. Also in Mignes, Patrologia Latina, Vol. 50. Hallam calls the text "the celebrated rule." It is all now remembered of St. V. by most educated men. It is shown to be of no practical value in an able criticism by Sir G. C. Lewis, *Influence of Authority in Matters of Opinion*, 2nd ed., 1875, p. 57. Mr Gladstone reviewed this work of Lewis, *Nineteenth Century* March, 1877.

{231b} Hugo of St. Victor (1097-1141), a celebrated Mystic born at Ypres in Flanders. His collected works first appeared at Rouen in 1648.

{231c} St. Bonaventura (A.D. 1221-1274). Born at Bagnarea, near Orvieto, in Tuscany, became a Franciscan monk and afterwards a Professor of Theology at Paris, where he gained the title of the "Seraphic Doctor." Made a Cardinal by Pope Gregory X, who sent him as his Legate to the Council at Lyons, where he died. In 1482 he was canonized. His writings appeared at Rome in 1588-96.

{231d} St. Thomas Aquinas (A.D. 1225-1274). The Angelic Doctor was born at the castle of Rocca-Secca near Aquino, between Rome and Naples. Entered the Dominican Order in 1243. Went to Paris in 1252 and attained great distinction as a theologian. His *Summa Theologiae* was followed by his *Summa contra Gentiles*. His works were first collected in 17 volumes in 1570. Aquinas was canonized in 1323.

{232a} Dante (A.D. 1265-1321). The *Divina Commedia* has been translated into English by many scholars. The best known version is the poetical renderings of H. F. Cary (1772-1844) and W. W. Longfellow (1807- 1882) and the prose translations (the "Inferno" only) of John Carlyle (1801-79) and A. J. Butler in whose three volumes of the "Purgatory," "Paradise" and "Inferno" the original Italian may be studied side by side with the translation.

{232b} Raymund of Sabunde, a physician of Toulouse of the fifteenth century. He published his *Theologia naturalis* at Strassburg in 1496. "I found the concerts of the author to be excellent, the contexture of his works well followed, and his project full of pietie" writes Montaigne in telling us of his father's request that he should translate Sabunde's *Theologia naturalis*. Florio's Translation. Book II, Ch. XII.

{232c} Nicholas of Cusa (A.D. 1401-1464) was born at Kues on the Moselle. His *De Concordantia Catholica* was a treatise in favour of the Councils of the Church and against the authority of the Pope. He was made a Cardinal by Pope Nicholas V.

{232d} Edward Reuss (1804-1891), a professor of Theology, who was born at Strassburg. Published his *History of the New Testament* in 1842 and his *History of the Old Testament* in 1881. *The Bible, a new translation with Introduction and Commentaries*, appeared in 19 volumes between 1874 and 1881.

{233a} Pascal, Blaise (1623-1662). Born at Clermont-Ferrand in Auvergne. His *Letters to a Provincial*, written in 1656-7, made his fame by their attack on the Jesuists. His *Pensees* appeared after his death, in 1669, and they have reappeared in many forms, "edited" by many schools of thought. The edition edited by Ernest Havet (1813-1889) was published in 1852.

{233b} Malebranche, Nicolas (1638-1715). Born in Paris. The works of Descartes drew him to philosophy. The famous dictum, "Malebranche saw all things in God," had reference to his treatise, *De la Recherche de la Verite*, first published in 1674.

{233c} Baader, Franz (1765-1841). A speculative philosopher and theologian, born at Munich, who endeavoured to reconcile the tenets of the Church of Rome with philosophy. Of his many works his *Vorlesungen uber Spekulative Dogmatik* is here selected. It appeared between 1828 and 1838 in five parts.

{233d} Molitor, Franz Joseph (1779-1860). A philosophical writer, born near Frankfurt. His *Philosophie der Geschichte, oder uber Tradition* was published in 4 volumes between 1827 and 1853.

{233e} Astie, Jean Frederic (1822-1894). A French Protestant theologian, who held a Chair of Theology in New York from 1848 to 1853. In 1856 became a Professor in Switzerland. He published his *Esprit d'Alexandre Vinet* at Paris in 1861. In 1882 appeared his *Le Vinet de la legende et celui de l'histoire*.

{234a} Punjer, Bernard (1850-1884). A theologian whose *Geschichte der Religions-philosophie* was much the vogue with theological students at the time of its publication in 1880. It was reissued in 1887 in an English translation by W. Hastie, under the title, *History of the Christian Philosophy of Religion from the Reformation to Kant*. Punjer also wrote *Die Religionslehre Kant's*, published at Jena in 1874.

{234b} Rothe, Richard (1799-1867). A Protestant theologian. Was for a time preacher to the Prussian Embassy in Rome, and afterwards in succession Professor of Theology at Wittenberg, at Heidelberg, and at Bonn. His *Theologische Ethik* appeared at Wittenberg in 3 volumes between 1845 and 1848.

{234c} Martensen, Hans Lassen (1808-1884). A Danish theologian, born at Fleusburg and died at Copenhagen, where he was long a Professor of Theology. He became Bishop of Zeeland. *Die Christliche Ethik* was one of many works by him. He also wrote *Die Christliche Dogmatik, Die Christliche Taufe*, and a *Life of Jakob Bohme*.

{234d} Oettingen, Alexander von (1827-1905). A theologian and statistician principally associated with Dorpat in Livonia, where he studied from 1845 to 1849. He became Professor of Theology at its famous University. His principal book is entitled, *Die Moralstatistik in ihrer Bedeutung für eine Sozialethik.*

{234e} Hartmann, Karl Robert Eduard von (1842-1906). Born in Berlin, the son of General Robert von Hartmann, and served for some time in the Artillery of the German Army. He has written many philosophical works. His *Phanomenologie des sittlichlen Bewusstseins* was published in Berlin in 1879.

{235a} Leibniz, Gottfried Wilhelm (1646-1716). Born at Leipzig and died at Hanover. Visited Paris and London, and became acquainted with Boyle and Newton. In 1676 appointed to a librarianship at Hanover. His philosophical views are mainly derived from his letters. The edition of the *Letters*, edited by Ouno Klopp (1822-1903), appeared at Hanover between 1862 and 1884 in 11 volumes.

{235b} Brandis, Christian August (1790-1867). A philosopher and philologist, born in Hildesheim, studied in Gottingen and Kiel. Accompanied Niebuhr as Secretary to the Embassy to Rome in 1816. In 1822 became Professor of Philosophy in Bonn. His *Handbuch der Geschichte der griechischromischen Philosophie*, doubtless here referred to by Lord Acton, was published in Berlin at long intervals (1835-66) in 3 volumes.

{235c} Fischer, Kuno (1824-1907). Born at Sandewalde in Silesia. Deprived of his professorship of philosophy at Heidelberg by the Baden Government in 1853 on account of charge of Pantheism, but recalled to Heidelberg in 1872. His principal book is *Geschichte der Neuern Philosophie* (1852-1903). His *Franz Baco von Verulam* appeared in 1856, and *Francis Bacon und seine Schule* made the 10th volume of his *Geschichte.*

{235d} Zeller, Eduard (1814-still living). Theologian and

historian of philosophy. Studied at Tubingen and Berlin, became Professor of Theology at Berne, afterwards held chairs successively at Heidelberg and Berlin. His many works include *The Philosophy of Ancient Greece*, *Platonic Studies* and *Zwingli's Theological System*.

{236a} Bartholomess, Christian (1815-1856). A French philosopher, born at Geiselbronn in Alsace. From 1853 Professor of Philosophy at Strassburg. Died at Nuremberg. Wrote a *Life of Giordano Bruno*, and *Philosophical History of the Prussian Academy*, *particularly under Frederick the Great*, as well as the *Histoire critique des doctrines religieuses de la philosophie moderne*, published in 2 volumes in 1855.

{236b} Madame Guyon (1648-1717) was born at Montargis in France, and her maiden name was Jeanne Marie Bouvieres de la Mothe. She married at 16 years of age Jacques Guyon. Left a widow, she devoted herself to a religious mysticism which raised up endless controversies during the succeeding years. She was compelled to leave Geneva because her doctrines were declared to be heretical. She was imprisoned in the Bastile from 1695 to 1702. Her works are contained in 39 volumes.

{236c} Ritschl, Albrecht (1822-1889). Professor of Theology, born in Berlin, died in Gottingen. Became Professor of Theology in Bonn and later in Gottingen. He wrote many books. His *Die Entstehung der altkatholischen Kirche* first appeared in 1850.

{236d} Loening, Edgar (1843- still living), was born in Paris. Has held professorial chairs at Strassburg, Dorpat, Rostock, and at Halle. His *Geschichte des deutschen Kirchenrechts* first appeared in 1878.

{237a} Baur, Ferdinand Christian (1792-1860). Born at Schmiden, near Kannstatt. Held various theological chairs before that of Tubingen, which he occupied from 1826 until his death. He wrote a great number of theological works, of which his *Vorlesungen uber die christliche Dogmengeschichte* was published in Leipzig in 3 volumes between 1865 and 1867.

{237b} Fenelon, Francois de Salignac de la Mothe (1651-1715). Born in Perigord in France, and famous alike as a divine and as a man of letters, his *Telemaque* living in literature. His controversy over Madame Guyon is well known. Louis XIV made him preceptor to his grandson, the Duke of Burgundy, and later Archbishop of Cambrai. His *Correspondence* was published between 1727 and 1729 in 11 volumes.

{237c} Newman, John Henry (1801-1890). A famous Cardinal of the Church of Rome; born in London, educated at Trinity College, Oxford; first Vicar of St. Mary's, Oxford; took part in the Tractarian Movement with some of the *Tracts for the Times*. His *Apologia pro Vita Sua* appeared in 1864, his *Dream of Gerontius* in 1865. There is no *Theory of Development* by Newman. His *Essay on the Development of Christian Doctrine* appeared in 1845, and was replied to by the Rev. J. B. Mozley in a volume bearing the title *The Theory of Development*.

{237d} Mozley, James Bowling (1813-1878). A Church of England divine; born at Gainsborough, educated at Oriel College, Oxford; became Vicar of Old Shoreham, Canon of Worcester, and, in 1871, Regius Professor of Divinity at Oxford. His *Oxford University Sermons* appeared in 1876.

{238a} Schneckenburger, Matthias (1804-1848). A Protestant theologian; born at Thalheim and died in Berne, where he was for a time Professor of Theology at the newly founded University. His *Vergleichende Darstellung des lutherischen und reformierten Lehrbegriffs* was published in Stuttgart in 2 volumes in 1855.

{238b} Hundeshagen, Karl Bernhard (1810-1872). A Protestant theologian who held a professorship in Berne, later in Heidelberg and finally in Bonn, where he died. His many works included one upon the Conflict between the Lutheran, the Calvinistic, and the Zwinglian Churches. His *Beitrage zur Kirchenverfassungsgeschichte und Kirchenpolitik insbesondere des Protestantismus* was published at Wiesbaden in 1864 in 1 volume.

{238c} Schweizer, Alexander (1808-1888). A theologian and preacher who studied in Zurich and Berlin. He wrote his *Autobiography* which was published in Zurich the year after his death. His book, *Die protestantischen Centraldogmen innerhalb der reformierten Kirche*, appeared in Zurich in 2 volumes in 1854 and 1856.

{238d} Gass, Wilhelm (1813-1889). A Protestant theologian; born at Breslau and died in Heidelberg, where he held a theological chair. His best-known book is his *Geschichte der protestantischen Dogmatik*, published in Berlin between 1854 and 1867 in 4 volumes, and to this Lord Acton doubtless refers.

{238e} Cart, Jacques Louis (1826-probably still living). A Swiss pastor; born in Geneva; the author of many books, of which the one named by Lord Acton is fully entitled, *Histoire du mouvement religieux et ecclesiastique dans le canton de Vaud pendant la premiere moitie du XIXe siecle*. It appeared between 1871 and 1880 in 6 volumes.

{239a} Blondel, David (1590-1655). Born at Chalons-sur-

Marne in France; a learned theologian and historian who defended the Protestant position against the Catholics. Was Professor of History at Amsterdam. His *De la primaute de l'Eglise* appeared in 1641.

{239b} Le Blanc de Beaulieu, Louis (1614-1675). A French Protestant theologian who enjoyed the consideration of both parties and was approached by Turenne with a view to a reunion of the churches. His position was sustained before the Protestant Academy at Sedan with certain theses published under the title of *Theses Sedanenzes* in 1683.

{239c} Thiersch, Heinrich Wilhelm Josias (1817-1885). Born in Munich and died in Basle; held for a time a Professorship of Theology in Marburg, then became the principal pastor of the Irvingite Church in Germany, preaching in many cities. He wrote many books. His *Vorlesungen uber Katholizismus und Protestantismus* appeared first in 1846.

{239d} Mohler, Johann Adam (1796-1838). Born in Igersheim and died in Munich. A Catholic theologian and Professor of Theology at Tubingen. His *Neue Untersuchungen der Lehrgegensatze zwischen den Katholiken und Protestanten* was first published in Mainz in 1834.

{240a} Scherer, Edmond (1815-1889). A French theologian; born in Paris, died at Versailles. Was for a time in England, then Professor of Exegesis in Geneva. Was for many years a leader of the French Protestant Church. His *Melanges de critique religieuse* appeared in Paris in 1860.

{240b} Hooker, Richard (1554-1600). Born in Exeter. In 1584 was Rector of Drayton-Beauchamp, near Tring, and the following year became Master of the Temple. In 1591 became Vicar of Boscombe and sub-Dean of Salisbury. His *Laws of Ecclesiastical Polity* was published in 1594. In 1595 he removed to Bishopsbourne, near Canterbury, where he died.

{240c} Weingarten, Hermann (1834-1892). Protestant ecclesiastical historian, born in Berlin, where in 1868 he became a professor, later held chairs successively at Marberg and Breslau. His book *Die Revolutionskirchen Englands* appeared in 1868.

{240d} Kliefoth, Theodor Friedrich (1810-1895). A Lutheran theologian; born at Kirchow in Mecklenburg, and died at Schwerin, where he was for a time instructor to the Grand Duke of Mecklenburg-Schwerin, and held various offices in connexion with that state. He wrote many theological works. His *Acht Bucher von der Kirche* was published at Schwerin in 1 volume in 1854.

{240e} Laurent, Francois (1810-1887). Born in Luxemburg and died in Gent, where he long held a professorship. His principal work, *Etudes sur l'histoire de l'humanite, Histoire du droit des gens* was published in Brussels in 18 volumes between 1860 and 1870.

{241a} Ferrari, Guiseppe (1812-1876) was born in Milan, and died in Rome. Achieved fame as a philosophical historian. Held a chair at Turin and afterwards at Milan. As member of the Parliament of Piedmont he was an opponent of Cavour's policy of a United Italy. His principal book is entitled *Histoire des revolutions de l'Italie, ou Guelfes et Gibelins*, published in Paris in four volumes between 1856 and 1858.

{241b} Lange, Friedrich Albert (1828-1875). Philosopher and economic writer, born at Wald bei Solingen, died at Marburg. Held a professorial chair at Zurich and later at Marburg. His most famous book, the *Geschichte des*

Materialismus und Kritik seiner Bedentung in der Gegenwart, first appeared in 1866. It was published in England in 1878- 81 by Trubner in three volumes.

{241c} Guicciardini, Francesco (1483-1540), the Italian historian and statesman, was born at Florence. Undertook in 1512 an embassy from Florence to the Court of Ferdinand the Catholic, and learned diplomacy in Spain. In 1515 he entered the service of Pope Leo X. His principal book is his *History of Italy*. The *Istoria d'Italia* appeared in Florence in ten volumes between 1561 and 1564. His *Recordi Politici* consists of some 400 aphorisms on political and social topics and has been described by an Italian critic as "Italian corruption codified and elevated to a rule of life."

{241d} Duperron, Jacques Davy (1556-1618), a Cardinal of the Church, born at Saint Lo. He was a Court preacher under Henry III of France and denounced Elizabeth of England in a funeral sermon on Mary Stuart. It is told of him that he once demonstrated before the king the existence of God, and being complimented upon his irrefutable arguments, replied that he was prepared to bring equally good arguments to prove that God did not exist. He became Bishop of Evreux in 1591.

{242a} Richelieu, Cardinal—(Armand-Jean Du Plessis)—(1585-1642). The famous minister of Louis XIII; born in Paris, of a noble family of Poitou. Was made Bishop of Lucon by Henry IV at the age of twenty-two. Became Almoner to Marie de Medici, the Regent of France. Was elected a Cardinal in 1622. He wrote many books, including theological works, tragedies, and his own Memoirs. The authenticity of his *Testament politique* was disputed by Voltaire.

{242b} Harrington, James (1611-1677) was born at Upton,

Northamptonshire; was educated at Trinity College, Cambridge. He travelled on the Continent, but was back in England at the time of the Civil War, in which, however, he took no part. He published his *Oceana* in 1656. He is buried in St. Margaret's Church, Westminster, next to the tomb of Sir Walter Raleigh. His *Writings* in an edition issued in 1737 by Millar contained twenty separate treatises in addition to *Oceana*, but concerned with that book.

{242c} Mignet, Francois Auguste Marie (1796-1884). The historian; was born at Aix and died in Paris. Published his *History of the French Revolution* in 1824. His *Negociations relatives a la succession d'Espagne* appeared in 4 volumes between 1836 and 1842. He also wrote a *Life of Franklin*, a *History of Mary Stuart*, and many other works.

{243a} Rousseau, Jean Jacques (1712-1778), the famous writer, was born in Geneva and died at Ermenonville. Much of his life story has been told in his incomparable *Confessions*. In 1759 he published *Nouvelle Heloise*; in 1762, *L'Emile ou de l'Education*. His *Considerations sur la Pologne* was written by Rousseau in 1769 in response to an application to apply his own theories to a scheme for the renovation of the government of Poland, in which land anarchy was then at its height. Mr. John Morley (*Rousseau*, Vol. II) dismisses the pamphlet with a contemptuous line.

{243b} Foncin, Pierre (1841- still living). A French Professor of History; born at Limoges, and has long held important official positions in connexion with education. He has written many books, including an *Atlas Historique*. His *Essai sur le ministere Turgot* appeared in 1876, and obtained a prize from the French Academy.

{243c} Burke, Edmund (1729-1797), the famous statesman, was born in Dublin and died at Beaconsfield, Bucks, where he was buried. His *Vindication of Natural Society* appeared in 1756. Burke entered Parliament for Wendover in 1765, sat for Bristol, 1774-80, and Malton, 1780-94. His *Collected Works* first appeared in 1792-1827 in 8 volumes, the first three of which were issued in his lifetime; his *Collected Works and Correspondence* was published in 8 volumes in 1852, but the *Correspondence* had appeared separately in 4 volumes in 1844.

{243d} Las Cases, Emmanuel Augustine Dieudonne Marir Joseph (1766-1842). Educated at the Military School in Paris but entered the French navy; emigrated at the Revolution; fought at Quiberon; taught French in London; published in 1802 his *Atlas historique et geographique* under the pseudonym of "Le Sage." On his return to France he came under the notice of Napoleon, who made him a Count of the Empire and sent him upon several important missions. During the Emperor's exile in Elba he again went to England. He returned during the Hundred Days and accompanied Napoleon to St. Helena. Here he recorded day by day the conversations of the great exile. At the end of eighteen months he was exiled by Sir Hudson Lowe to the Cape of Good Hope. He returned to France after the death of Napoleon and became a Deputy under Louis Philippe. His *Memorial de Sainte-Helene*, published in 1823-1824, secured a great success.

{244a} Holtzendorff, Franz von (1829-1889), was Professor of Jurisprudence first at Berlin and afterwards at Munich, where he died. He wrote many books concerned with crime and its punishment, with the prison systems of the world, etc. His *Enzyklopadie der Rechtswissenschaft in systematischer und alphabetischer Bearbeitung* was first published at Leipzig in 1870 and 1871.

{244b} Jhering, Rudolph von (1818-1892), was for a time

professor at Basle, Rostock, Kiel and Vienna. His *Geist des romischen Rechts auf den verschiedenen Stufen seiner Entwickelung* appeared in Leipzig between 1852 and 1865, and is counted a classic in jurisprudence.

{244c} Geib, Karl Gustav (1808-1864). An eminent criminologist. Was a Professor of Zurich and afterwards of Tubingen, where he died. Wrote many books, of which the most important was his *Geschichte des romischen Kriminalprozesses bis zum Tode Justinians* in 1842. His *Lehrbuch des deutschen Strafrechts* appeared in 1861 and 1862, but was never completed.

{245a} Maine, Sir Henry James Sumner (1822-1888). Jurist; born in Kelso, Scotland; educated at Christ's Hospital, London, and at Pembroke College, Cambridge; was Regius Professor of Civil Law at Cambridge, 1847- 54. In 1862 he became a legal member of Council in India and held the office for seven years. In 1871 he became a K.C.S.I. and had a seat on the Indian Council. In 1877 he was elected Master of Trinity Hall, Cambridge, and in 1887 became Whewell Professor of International Law at Cambridge. He died at Cannes. His principal work is his *Ancient Law: its Connexion with the Early History of Society and its Relation to Modern Ideas*, first published in 1861.

{245b} Gierke, Otto Friedrich (1841- still living), was born in Stettin; was Professor of Law in Breslau, Heidelberg and Berlin successively. Served in the Franco-German War of 1870. His principal work, *Das deutsche Genossenschaftsrecht*, appeared in 3 volumes in Berlin, the first in 1868, the third in 1881.

{245c} Stahl, Friedrich Julius (1802-1861), was born in Munich of Jewish parents, died in Bruckenau. Held chairs of law and jurisprudence in Berlin and other cities, and wrote many books. His *Die Philosophie des Rechts und geschichtlicher Ansicht* appeared at Heidelberg in 2 volumes in 1830 and 1837.

{246a} Gentz, Friedrich von (1764-1832). A distinguished publicist and statesman; born in Breslau, died at Weinhaus, near Vienna; studied Jurisprudence in Konigsberg. One of his earliest literary efforts was a translation of Burke's *Reflections upon the French Revolution*. Played a very considerable part in the combination of the powers of Europe against Napoleon in 1809-15. He was the author of many books. His *Briefewechsel mit Adam Muller* was published in Stuttgart in 1857—long after his death.

{246b} Vollgraff, Karl Friedrich (1794-1863), was for a time Professor of Jurisprudence at Marburg, where he died. His two most important books were: (1) *Der Systeme der praktischen Politik im Abendlande*; (2) *Erster Versuch einer Begrundung der allgemeinen Ethnologie durch die Anthropologie und der Staats und Rechts Philosophie durch die Ethnologie oder Nationalitat der Volker*, published in 4 volumes in 1851 to 1855. It is in this last volume that a section is devoted to Polignosie.

{246c} Frantz, Konstantin (1817-1891). Distinguished publicist; born at Halberstadt and died at Blasewitz, near Dresden, where he made his home for many years. Was for a time German Consul in Spain. His great doctrine laid down in his *Die Weltpolitik*, 1883, was the union of Central Europe against the growing power of Russia and the United States of America. His *Kritik aller Parteien* was published in Berlin in 1862.

{246d} Maistre, Joseph Marie Comte de (1753-1821). A distinguished French publicist; born at Chambery; studied at the University of Turin. Lived for some years at Lausanne, where he published in 1796 his *Considerations sur la Revolution francaise.*

{247a} Donoso Cortes, Jean Francois (1809-1853). A famous Spanish publicist; born in Estremadura; played a considerable part in Spanish affairs under Marie-Christine and Queen Isabella. Was for a time Spanish Ambassador to Berlin, and later to France, where he died in Paris. He wrote much upon such questions as the Catholic Church and Socialism.

{247b} Perin, Henri Charles Xavier (1815-), a Belgium economist, born at Mons; became an advocate at Brussels and also Professor of Political Economy in that city. His book *De la Richesse dans les Societes Chretiennes* appeared in Paris in 2 volumes in 1861.

{247c} Le Play, Pierre Guillaume Frederic (1806-1882). Born at Honfleur. He directed the organization of the Paris International Exhibitions of 1855 and 1867. He wrote many books. His *La reforme sociale en France deduite de l'observation comparee des peuples Europeens* was published in two volumes in 1864.

{247d} Riehl, Wilhelm Heinrich (1823-1897). A well-known author; born at Biebrich-am-Rhein, died in Munich. He was associated with several German newspapers, and edited from 1848 to 1851 the *Nassauische Allgemeine Zeitung*, from 1851 to 1853 the *Augsburger Allgemeine Zeitung*, and afterwards became a Professor of Literature at Munich. In 1885 he became the director of the Bavarian National Museum. He wrote many books, the one referred to by Lord Acton having been published in 1851 under the title of *Die burgerliche Gesellschaft.*

{248a} Sismondi, Jean Charles Leonard Sismonde de (1773-

1842), the distinguished historian of the Italian republics, was born at Geneva of an Italian family originally from Pisa. He resided for a time in England. His famous book the *Histoire des Republiques Italiennes de Moyen-Age* appeared between 1807 and 1818 in 16 volumes. His *Etudes sur les Constitutions des Peuples Libres*, was one of many other books.

{248b} Rossi, Pellegrino Luigi Odoardo (1787-1848). An Italian publicist; born at Carrara. Keenly sympathized with the French Revolution and served under Murat in the Hundred Days, after which he fled to Geneva. In later years he became a nationalized Frenchman, occupied a Chair of Constitutional Law, and finally became a peer. As Comte Rossi he went on a special embassy to Rome. He was assassinated in that city during the troubles of 1848. His *Traite du Droit Constitutionnel* appeared in 2 volumes.

{248c} Barante, Aimable Guillaume Prosper Brugiere, baron de (1782-1868), historian and politician, was born at Riom. He was made a Counciller of State by Louis XVIII in 1815, and a peer of France in 1819. He was elected a member of the French Academy in 1828. Under Louis Philippe he became Ambassador first at Turin and afterwards at St. Petersburg. After the revolution of 1848 he devoted himself entirely to literature. He wrote many historical and literary studies, and translated the works of Schiller into French. His *Vie politique de Royer-Collard* has several times been reprinted.

{249a} Duvergier de Hauranne, Prosper (1798-1881), was a distinguished French publicist, born at Rouen. He was parliamentary deputy for Sancerre in 1831 and took part in most of the political struggles of the following twenty years. He was exiled from France at the time of the *Coup d'Etat*, but returned during the reign of Napoleon III. Henceforth he devoted himself exclusively to historical studies. His *Histoire du gouvernement parlementaire en France*, published in 1870, secured his election to the French Academy.

{249b} Madison, James (1751-1836). The fourth President of the United States; born at Port Conway, Virginia. Acted with Jay and Hamilton in the Convention which framed the Constitution and wrote with them *The Federalist.* He had two terms of office—between 1809 and 1817—as President. He died at Montpelier, Virginia. His *Debates of the Congress of Confederation* was published in Elliot's "Debates on the State Conventions," 4 vols., Philadelphia, 1861.

{249c} Hamilton, Alexander (1757-1804). A great American statesman, who served in Washington's army, and after the war became eminent as a lawyer in New York. He wrote fifty-one out of the eighty-five essays of *The Federalist.* He was appointed Secretary of the Treasury to the United States in 1789. He was mortally wounded in a duel by Aaron Burr in 1804. His influence upon the American Constitution gives him a great place in the annals of the Republic.

{249d} Calhoun, John Campbell (1782-1850). An American statesman; born in Abbeville County, South Carolina and studied at Yale. As a Member of Congress he supported the war with Great Britain in 1812-15. He was twice Vice-President of the United States. He died at Washington. A *Disquisition on Government* and a *Discourse on the Constitution and Government of the United States* were written in the last months of his life. His *Collected Works* appeared in 1853-4.

{250a} Dumont, Pierre Etienne Louis (1759-1829). A great publicist; born in Geneva, and principally known in England by his association with Bentham, to whom he acted as an editor and interpreter. Lived much in Paris, St. Petersburg, and, above all, in London, where he knew Fox, Sheridan, and other famous men, and taught the children of Lord Shelburne. Dumont's *Sophismes Anarchiques* appears in Bentham's *Collected Works* as *Anarchical Fallacies*.

{250b} Quinet, Edgar (1803-1875). French historian and philosopher; born at Borg and died in Paris. His epic poem of *Ahasuerus* was placed upon the Index. Of his many books his *La Revolution Francaise* is the best known. It was written in Switzerland, where he was an exile during the reign of Napoleon III. He returned to France in 1870.

{250c} Stein, Lorenz von (1815-1890). Writer on economics, studied in Kiel and in Jena. In 1855 he became Professor of International Law in Vienna. He wrote books on statecraft and international law. His work entitled *Der Sozialismus und Kommunismus des heutigen Frankreich* appeared in Leipzig in 1843.

{251a} Lassalle, Ferdinand (1825-1864), the famous social democrat, was of Jewish birth; born at Breslau. He took part in the revolution of 1848 and received six months' imprisonment. He was wounded in a duel at Geneva over a love affair and died two days later. His *System der Erworbenen Rechte* appeared in 1861.

{251b} Thonissen, Jean Joseph (1817-1891). A distinguished jurist; born in Belgium. He studied at Liege and in Paris; became a Professor of the Catholic University of Louvain; afterwards became a Minister of State. Of his many works his *Socialisme depuis l'antiquite jusqu'a la constitution francaise de 1852* is best known.

{251c} Considerant, Victor (1808-1894). Born at Salins, and, after the Revolution of 1848, entered the Chamber of Deputies. He crossed to America to found a colony in Texas, but ruined himself by the experiment. He returned to France in 1869. He was the author of many socialistic treatises.

{251d} Roscher, Wilhelm (1817-1894), economist, was born in Hanover. Held a chair first in Gottingen and afterwards in Leipzig, where he died. His *Geschichte der Nationalokonomik in Deutschland* appeared in Munich in 1874.

{251e} Mill, John Stuart (1806-1873), the famous publicist and author, was born in London, and educated by his father, James Mill (1773-1836). He served in the India Office, 1823-58; he was M.P. for Westminster, 1865- 68. His works include the *Principles of Political Economy*, 1848; the *Essay on Liberty*, 1859, and the *System of Logic*, which first appeared in 1843.

{252a} Coleridge, Samuel Taylor (1772-1834), poet and critic, was born at Ottery St. Mary, Devonshire; educated at Christ's Hospital, London, and at Jesus College, Cambridge. In the volume of *Lyrical Ballads* by Wordsworth of 1798 Coleridge contributed the *Ancient Mariner*, and he was to make his greatest reputation by this and other poems. His best prose work was his *Biographia Literaria* (1817). His *Aids to Reflection* was first published in 1825.

{252b} Radowitz, Joseph Maria von (1797-1853). A Prussian general and statesman; born in Blankenberg and died in Berlin. Fought in the Napoleonic wars and was wounded at the battle of Leipzig. Afterwards served as Ambassador to various German Courts. He wrote several treatises bearing upon current affairs, and his *Fragments* form Vols. IV and V of his *Collected Works* in 5 volumes, which were issued in Berlin in 1852-53.

{252c} Gioberti, Vincent (1801-1852). An Italian statesman and philosopher; born in Turin, where he afterwards became

Professor of Theology. Was for a time Court Chaplain, but his liberal views led to exile, and he retired first to Paris, then to Brussels. Afterwards became famous as a neo-Catholic with his attempt to combine faith with science and art, and urged the independence and the unity of Italy. His *Jesuite moderne*, published in 1847, created a sensation. After some years of home politics he was appointed by King Victor Emmanuel as Ambassador to Paris. It is noteworthy in the light of Lord Acton's recommendation of his *Pensieri* that his works have been placed on the Index.

{253a} Humboldt, Friedrich Heinrich Alexander Baron von (1769-1859), the great naturalist, was born and died in Berlin, and studied at Frankfort- on-the-Oder, Berlin and Gottingen; he spent five years (1799-1804) in exploring South America, and in 1829 travelled through Central Asia. His *Kosmos* appeared between 1845 and 1858 in 4 volumes.

{253b} De Candolle, Alphonse de (1806-1893). The son of the celebrated botanist, Augustin Pyramus de Candolle, and was himself a professor of that science at Geneva. His *Histoire des sciences et des savants depuis deux siecles* appeared in 1873.

{253c} Darwin, Charles Robert (1809-1882), the great naturalist and discoverer of natural selection, was born at Shrewsbury, where he was educated at the Grammar School, at Edinburgh University, and at Christ's College, Cambridge. His most famous book, *The Origin of Species by means of Natural Selection*, was first published in 1859.

{253d} Littre, Maximilien Paul Emile (1801-1884), the famous lexicographer whose *Dictionnaire de la langue francaise* gave him a world-wide reputation. He was born in Paris. He associated himself with Auguste Comte and the *Positive Philosophy*, and contributed many volumes in support of Comte's standpoint.

{253e} Cournot, Antoine Augustin (1801-1877). Born at Gray in Savoy; wrote many mathematical treatises. His *Traite de l'enchainement des idees fondamentales dans les sciences et dans l'histoire* was published in 2 volumes.

{254} This was a most comprehensive addition, and fully makes up for the abrupt termination of the list of the hundred best books with two omissions. The omission of the book numbered 88 will also have been remarked. There are probably a hundred "Monatschriften der Wissenschaftlichen Vereine" or magazines of scientific societies issued in Germany. Sperling's *Zeitschriften-Adressbuch* gives more than two columns of these.

{260a} The Bible can be best read in paragraph form from the Eversley edition, published by the Macmillans, or from the Temple Bible, issued by J. M. Dent—the latter an edition for the pocket. The translation of 1610 is literature and has made literature. The revised translation of our own day has neither characteristic. Something can be said for the Douay Bible in this connexion. It was published in Douay in the same year as the Protestant version appeared—1610. Certain words from it, such as "Threnes" for "Lamentations" as the Threnes of Jeremiah, have a poetical quality that deserved survival.

{260b} The Iliad may be read in a hundred verse translations of which those by Pope and Cowper are the best known. Both these may be found in Bohn's Libraries (G. Bell & Sons); but the prose translation for which Mr. Lang and his friends are responsible (Macmillan) is for our generation far and away the best introduction to Homer for the non-Grecian.

{261a} Under the title of "The Athenian Drama," George Allen has published three fine volumes of the works of the Greek dramatists.

{261b} Dryden's translation of Virgil has been followed by many others both in prose and verse. There was one good prose version by C. Davidson recently issued in Laurie's Classical Library. An interesting translation of Virgil's *Georgics* into English verse was recently made by Lord Burghclere and published by John Murray. The young student, however, will do well to approach Virgil through Dryden. He will find the book in the Chandos Classics, or superbly printed in Professor Saintsbury's edition of *Dryden's Works*, Vol. XIV.

{261c} There have been many translations of Catullus. One, by Sir Richard Burton, was issued by Leonard Smithers in 1894. In Bohn's Library there is a prose translation by Walter K. Kelly. Professor Robinson Ellis made a verse translation that has been widely praised. Grant Allen translated the Attis in 1892. On the whole, the English verse translation by Sir Theodore Martin made in 1861 (Blackwood & Son) is far and away the best suited for a first acquaintance with this the 'tenderest of Roman Poets.'

{261d} Horace has been made the subject of many translations. Perhaps there are fifty now available. John Conington's edition of his complete works, two volumes (Bell), is well known. The best introduction to Horace for the young student is in Sir Theodore Martin's translation, two volumes (Blackwood), and a volume by the same author entitled *Horace* in "Ancient Classics for English Readers" (Blackwood) is a charming little book.

{262a} Dante's *Divine Comedy* as translated by Henry Francis Cary (1772- 1844) has been described by Mr. Ruskin as better reading than Milton's "Paradise Lost." James Russell Lowell, with true patriotism, declared that his countrymen Longfellow's translation (Routledge) was the best. Something may be said for the prose translation by Dr. John Carlyle of the *Inferno* (Bell) and for Mr. A. J. Butler's prose translation of the whole of the *Divine Comedy* in three volumes (Macmillan). Other translations which have had a great vogue are by Wright and Dean Plumptre. The best books on Dante are those by Dr. Edward Moore (Clarendon Press). Cary's translation can be obtained in one volume in Bohn's Library (Bell) or in the Chandos Classics (Warne).

{262b} I contend that while most of the poets are self-contained in a single volume, Shakspere's plays are best enjoyed as separate entities. Certainly each of them has a library attached to it, and it is quite profitable to read Hamlet in Mr. Horace Howard Furness's edition (Lippincott) with a multitude of criticisms of the play bound up with the text of Hamlet. But Hamlet should be read first in the Temple Shakspere (Dent) or in the Arden Shakspere (Methuen). To this last there is an admirable introduction by Professor Dowden.

{262c} Chaucer's *Canterbury Tales* should be read in Mr. Alfred W. Pollard's edition, which forms two volumes of the "Eversley Library" (Macmillan). The "Tales" may be obtained in cheaper form in the *Chaucer* of the Aldine Poets (Bell), of which I have grateful memories, having first read "Chaucer" in these little volumes. The enthusiast will obtain the Complete Works of Chaucer edited for the Clarendon Press by Professor W. W. Skeat.

{263a} FitzGerald's *Omar Khayyam* can be obtained in its four versions, each of which has its merits, only from the Macmillans, who publish it in many forms. The edition in the Golden Treasury Series may be particularly commended.

The present writer has written an introduction to a sixpenny edition of the first version. It is published by William Heinemann.

{263b} Goethe's *Faust* has been translated in many forms. Certainly Anster's version (Sampson Low) is the most vivacious. Anna Swanwick, Sir Theodore Martin and Bayard Taylor's translations have about equal merit.

{263c} Shelley's *Poetical Works* should be read in the one volume issued in green cloth by the Macmillans, with an introduction by Edward Dowden, or in the Oxford Poets (Henry Froude), with an introduction by H. Buxton Forman, but perhaps the best edition is that of the Clarendon Press with an introduction by Thomas Hutchinson. Mr. Forman's library edition of *Shelley's Complete Works* is the desire of all collectors.

{263d} *Byron's Poetical Works*, edited by Ernest Coleridge, form seven volumes of John Murray's edition of Byron's *Works* in thirteen volumes. There is not a good one-volume Byron. I particularly commend the three- volume edition (George Newnes).

{264a} Wordsworth may be read in his entirety in the sixteen volumes of *Prose and Poetry* edited by William Knight in the Eversley Library (Macmillan). The same publisher issues an admirable *Wordsworth* in one volume, edited, with an introduction by John Morley. But the first approach to Wordsworth's verse should be made through Matthew Arnold's *Select Poems* in the Golden Treasury Series (Macmillan).

{264b} *Keats's Works* are issued in one volume in the Oxford Poets (Froude), and in five shilling volumes by Gowans and Gray of Glasgow. Mr. Buxton Forman's annotations to this cheap edition exceed in value those attached to his more expensive "Library Edition," which, however, as with the *Shelley*, in eight volumes, is out of print.

{264c} The four volumes of Burns, with an introduction by W. E. Henley, are pleasant to read. They are published by Jack, of Edinburgh. The best single-volume *Burns* is that in the Globe Library (Macmillan), with an introduction by Alexander Smith.

{264d} There is no rival to the one-volume edition of *Coleridge's Poems*, with an introduction by J. Dykes Campbell, published by Macmillan. Mr. Dykes Campbell's biography of Coleridge should also be read. The prose works of Coleridge are obtainable in Bohn's Library. The fortunate book lover has many in Pickering editions.

{264e} *Cowper's Complete Works* are acquired for a modest sum of the second-hand bookseller in Southey's sixteen-volume edition. The two best one-volume issues of the *Poems* are the Globe Library Edition with an introduction by Canon Benham (Macmillan), and *Cowper's Complete Poems* with an introduction by J. C. Bailey (Methuen). The best of the letters are contained in a volume in the Golden Treasury Series, with an introduction by Mrs. Oliphant. *The Complete Letters of Cowper*, edited by Thomas Wright, have been published by Hodder & Stoughton in four volumes.

{265a} *Crabbe's Works*, in eight volumes, with biography by his son, may be obtained very cheaply from the second-hand book seller. With all the merits of both *Works* and *Life* they have not been reprinted satisfactorily. The only good modern edition of *Crabbe's Poems* is in three volumes published by the Cambridge University Press, edited by A. W. Ward.

{265b} The best one-volume *Tennyson* is issued by the Macmillans, who still hold certain copyrights. The Library Edition of *Tennyson*, with the Biography included in the twelve volumes, is a desirable acquisition.

{265c} Not all the sixteen volumes of the Library Edition of *Browning* pay for perusal. The most convenient form is that of the two-volume edition (Smith, Elder & Co.), with notes by Augustine Birrell.

{265d} *Milton's Poetical Works* as annotated by David Masson (Macmillan) make the standard library edition, and the same publishers have given us the best one-volume *Milton* in the Globe Library, with an introduction by Professor Masson, Milton's one effective biographer.

{266a} *The Arabian Nights' Entertainments* is first introduced to us all as a children's story-book. Tennyson has placed on record his own early memories:—

"In sooth it was a goodly time,
For it was in the golden prime
Of good Haroun Alraschid."

But the collector of the hundred best books will do well to read the *Arabian Nights* in the translation by Edward William Lane, edited by Stanley Lane Poole, in 4 volumes, for George Bell & Sons.

{266b} The most satisfactory translation of Cervantes's great romance is that made by John Ormesby, revised and edited by James Fitzmaurice-Kelly, published by Gowans & Gray in 4 shilling volumes.

{266c} *The Pilgrim's Progress* is presented in a hundred forms. The present writer first read it in a penny edition. It should be possessed by the book-lover in a volume of the Cambridge English Classics, in which *Grace Abounding* and *The Pilgrim's Progress* are given together, edited by Dr. John Brown, and published by the Cambridge University Press.

{266d} Schoolboys, notwithstanding Macaulay, usually know but few good books, but every schoolboy knows Defoe's *Robinson Crusoe* in one form or another. The maker of a library will prefer it as a Volume of Defoe's *Works* (J. M. Dent), or as Volume VII of Defoe's *Novels and Miscellaneous Works* (Bell & Sons). There are many good shilling editions of the book by itself, but Defoe should be read in many of his works and particularly in *Moll Flanders*.

{267a} As with *Robinson Crusoe*, *Gulliver's Travels* can be obtained in many cheap forms, but it is well that it should be obtained as Volume VIII of *Swift's Prose Works*, published in Bohn's Libraries by George Bell & Sons. There has not been a really good edition of Swift's works since Scott's monumental book.

{267b} *Clarissa* should be read in nine of the twenty volumes of Richardson's Novels, published by Chapman & Hall—a very dainty well-printed book. "I love these large, still books," said Lord Tennyson.

{267c} The greatest of all novels, *Tom Jones*, is obtainable in several Library Editions of Fielding's *Works*. A cheap well-printed form is that of the *Works of Henry Fielding* in 12 volumes, published by Gay & Bird. Here *The Story of Tom Jones a Foundling* is in 4 volumes. The book is in 2 volumes in Bohn's Library—an excellent edition.

{267d} Johnson's *Rasselas* has frequently been reprinted, but there is no edition for a book-lover at present in the bookshops. It is included in *Classic Tales* in a volume of Bohn's Standard Library. The wise course is to look out for one of the earlier editions with copper plates that are constantly to be found on second-hand bookstalls. But Johnson's *Works* should be bought in a fine octavo edition.

{268a} Goldsmith's *Vicar of Wakefield* should be possessed in the edition which Mr. Hugh Thomson has illustrated and Mr. Austin Dobson has edited for the Macmillans. There is a good edition of Goldsmith's *Works* in Bohn's Library.

{268b} Sterne's *Sentimental Journey* is also a volume for the second- hand bookstall, although that and the equally fine *Tristram Shandy* may be obtained in many pretty forms. I have two editions of Sterne's books, but they are both fine old copies.

{268c} There are two very good editions of Peacock's delightful romances. *Nightmare Abbey* forms a volume of J. M. Dent's edition in 9 volumes, edited by Dr. Garnett; and the whole of Peacock's remarkable stories are contained in a single volume of Newnes' "Thin Paper Classics."

{268d} Sir Walter Scott's novels are available in many forms equally worthy of a good library. The best is the edition published by Jack of Edinburgh. The Temple Library of Scott (J. M. Dent) may be commended for those who desire pocket volumes, while Mr. Andrew Lang's Introductions give an added value to an edition published by the Macmillans, Scott's twenty-eight novels are indispensable to every good library, and every reader will have his own favourite.

{268e} Balzac's novels are obtainable in a good translation by Ellen Marriage, edited by George Saintsbury, published in New York by the Macmillan Company and in London by J. M. Dent.

{269a} A translation of Dumas' novels in 48 volumes is published by Dent. *The Three Musketeers* is in 2 volumes. There are many cheap one volume editions.

{269b} Thackeray's *Vanity Fair* is pleasantly read in the edition of his novels published by J. M. Dent. His original publishers, Smith, Elder & Co., issue his works in many forms.

{269c} The best edition of Charlotte Bronte's *Villette* is that in the "Haworth Edition," published by Smith, Elder & Co., with an Introduction by Mrs. Humphry Ward.

{269d} Charles Dickens' novels, of which *David Copperfield* is generally pronounced to be the best, should be obtained in the "Oxford India Paper Dickens" (Chapman & Hall and Henry Frowde). A serviceable edition is that published by the Macmillans, with Introductions by Charles Dickens's son, but that edition still fails of *Our Mutual Friend* and *The Mystery of Edwin Drood*, of which the copyright is not yet exhausted.

{269e} Anthony Trollope's novels are being reissued, in England by John Lane and George Bell & Sons, and in America in a most attractive form by Dodd, Mead & Co. All three publishers have a good edition of *Barchester Towers*, Trollope's best novel.

{269f} Boccaccio's *Decameron* is in my library in many forms—in 3 volumes of the Villon Society's publications, translated by John Payne; in 2 handsome volumes issued by Laurence & Bullen; and in the Extra Volumes of Bohn's Library. There is a pretty edition available published by Gibbons in 3 volumes.

{270a} Emily Bronte's *Wuthering Heights* forms a volume of

the Haworth Edition of the Bronte novels, published by Smith, Elder & Co. It has an introduction by Mrs. Humphry Ward.

{270b} Charles Reade's *Cloister and the Hearth* is available in many forms. The pleasantest is in 4 volumes issued by Chatto & Windus, with an Introduction by Sir Walter Besant. There is a remarkable shilling edition issued by Collins of Glasgow.

{270c} Victor Hugo's *Les Miserables* may be most pleasantly read in the 10 volumes, translated by M. Jules Gray, published by J. M. Dent & Co.

{270d} Mrs. Gaskell's *Cranford* can be obtained in the six volume edition of that writer's works published by Smith, Elder & Co., with Introductions by Dr. A. W. Ward; in a volume illustrated by Hugh Thomson, with an Introduction by Mrs. Ritchie, published by the Macmillans, or in the World's Classics (Henry Frowde), where there is an additional chapter entitled, "The Cage at Cranford."

{270e} The translation of George Sand's *Consuelo* in my library is by Frank H. Potter, 4 volumes, Dodd, Mead & Co., New York.

{270f} Lever's *Charles O'Malley* I have as volumes of the *Complete Works* published by Downey. There is a pleasant edition in Nelson's "Pocket Library."

{271a} Macaulay's *History of England* is available in many attractive forms from the original publishers, the Longmans. There is a neat thin paper edition for the pocket in 5 volumes issued by Chatto & Windus.

{271b} For Carlyle's *Past and Present* I recommend the

Centenary Edition of Carlyle's *Works*, published by Chapman & Hall. There is an annotated edition of *Sartor Resartus* by J. A. S. Barrett (A. & C. Black), two annotated editions of *The French-Revolution*, one by Dr. Holland Rose (G. Bell & Sons), and an other by C. R. L. Fletcher, 3 volumes (Methuen), and an annotated edition of *The Cromwell Letters*, edited by S. C. Lomax, 3 volumes (Methuen). No publisher has yet attempted an annotated edition of *Past and Present*, but Sir Ernest Clarke's translation of *Jocelyn of Bragelond* (Chatto & Windus) may be commended as supplemental to Carlyle's most delightful book.

{271c} Motley's *Works* are available in 9 volumes of a Library Edition published by John Murray. A cheaper issue of the *Dutch Republic* is that in 3 volumes of the World's Classics, to which I have contributed a biographical introduction.

{271d} For many years the one standard edition of *Gibbon* was that published by John Murray, in 8 volumes, with notes by Dean Milman and others. It has been superseded by Professor Bury's annotated edition in 7 volumes (Methuen).

{272a} Plutarch's *Lives*, translated by A. Stewart and George Long, form 4 volumes of Bohn's Standard Library. There is a handy volume for the pocket in Dent's Temple Classics in 10 volumes, translated by Sir Thomas North.

{272b} Montaigne's *Essays* I have in three forms; in the Tudor Translations (David Nutt), where there is an Introduction to the 6 volumes of Sir Thomas North's translation by the Rt. Hon. George Wyndham; in Dent's Temple Classics, where John Florio's translation is given in 5 volumes. A much valued edition is that in 3 volumes, the translation by Charles Cotton, published by Reeves & Turner in 1877.

{272c} Steele's essays were written for the *Tatler* and the *Spectator* side by side with those of Addison. The best edition of *The Spectator* is that published in 8 volumes, edited by George A. Aitken for Nimmo, and of *The Tatler* that published in 4 volumes, edited also by Mr. Aitken for Duckworth & Co.

{272d} Lamb's *Essays of Elia* can be read in a volume of the Eversley Library (Macmillan), edited by Canon Ainger. The standard edition of Lamb's *Works* is that edited by Mr. E. V. Lucas, in 7 volumes, for Methuen. Mr. Lucas's biography of Lamb has superseded all others.

{272e} Thomas de Quincey's *Opium Eater* may be obtained as a volume of Newnes's Thin Paper Classics, in the World's Classics, or in Dent's Everyman's Library. But the *Complete Works* of De Quincey, in 16 volumes, edited by David Mason and published by A. & C. Black, should be in every library.

{273a} William Hazlitt never received the treatment he deserved until Mr. J. M. Dent issued in 1903 his *Collected Works*, in 13 volumes, edited by A. R. Waller and Arnold Glover. Of cheap reprints of Hazlitt I commend *The Spirit of the Age*, *Winterslow* and *Sketches and Essays*, three separate volumes of the World's Classics (Frowde).

{273b} George Borrow's *Lavengro* should only be read in Mr. John Murray's edition, as it there contains certain additional and valuable matter gathered from the original manuscript by William I. Knapp. The Library Edition of Borrow, in 6 volumes (Murray), may be particularly commended.

{273c} Emerson's *Complete Works* are published by the Routledges in 4 volumes, in which *Representative Men* may be found in Vol. II. Some may prefer the Eversley Library *Emerson*, which has an Introduction by John Morley. There are many cheap editions of about equal value.

{273d} Lander's *Imaginary Conversations* form six volumes of the complete *Landor*, edited by Charles G. Crump, and published in 10 volumes by J. M. Dent.

{273e} Matthew Arnold's *Essays in Criticism* is published by Macmillan. It also forms Vol. III of the Library Edition of his *Works* in 15 volumes. A "Second Series" has less significance.

{273f} *The Works of Herodotus*, published by the Macmillans, translated by George C. Macaulay, is the best edition for the general reader. Canon Rawlinson's *Herodotus*, published by John Murray, has had a longer life, but is now only published in an abridged form.

{274a} James Howell's *Familiar Letters*, or *Epistolae Ho Elianae*, should be read in the edition published in 2 volumes by David Nutt, with an Introduction by Joseph Jacobs.

{274b} *The History of Civilization*, by Henry Thomas Buckle, is in my library in the original 2 volumes published by Parker in 1857. It is now issued in 3 volumes in Longman's Silver Library, and in 3 volumes in the World's Classics.

{274c} *The History of Tacitus* should be read in the translation by Alfred John Church and William Jackson Brodripp. It is published by the Macmillans.

{274d} *Our Village*, by Mary Russell Mitford, is a collection of essays which in their completest form may be obtained in two volumes of Bohn's Library (Bell). The essential essays should be possessed in the edition published by the Macmillans—*Our Village*, by Mary Russell Mitford, with an Introduction by Anne Thackeray Ritchie, and one hundred illustrations by Hugh Thomson.

{274e} Green's *Short History of the English People* is published by the Macmillans in 1 volume, or illustrated in 4 volumes. The book was enlarged, but disimproved, under the title of *A History of the English People*, in 4 volumes, uniform with the *Conquest of England* and the *Making of England* by the same author.

{275a} Taine's *Ancient Regime* is a good introduction to the conditions which made the French Revolution. It forms the first volume of *Les Origines de la France Contemporaine*, and may be read in a translation by John Durand, published by Dalby, Isbister & Co. in 1877.

{275b} *The Life of Napoleon* has been written by many pens, in our own day most competently by Dr. Holland Rose (2 vols. Bell); but a good account of the Emperor, indispensable for some particulars and an undoubted classic, is that by de Bourrienne, Napoleon's private secretary, published in an English translation, in 4 volumes, by Bentley in 1836.

{275c} *Democracy in America*, by Alexis de Tocqueville, may be had in a translation by Henry Reeve, published in 2 volumes by the Longmans. Read also *A History of the United States* by C. Benjamin Andrews, 2 volumes (Smith, Elder), and above all the *American Commonwealth*, by James Bryce, 2 volumes (Macmillan).

{275d} *The Compleat Angler* of Isaac Walton may be purchased in many forms. I have a fine library edition edited by that prince of living anglers, Mr. R. B. Marston, called The Lea and Dove Edition, this being the 100th edition of the book (Sampson Low, 1888). I have also an edition edited by George A. B. Dewar, with an Introduction by Sir Edward Grey and Etchings by William Strang and D. Y. Cameron, 2 volumes (Freemantle), and a 1 volume edition published by Ingram & Cooke in the Illustrated Library.

{276a} There are many editions of Gilbert White's *Natural History of Selbourne* to be commended. Three that are in my library are (1) edited with an Introduction and Notes by L. C. Miall and W. Warde Fowler (Methuen); (2) edited with Notes by Grant Allen, illustrated by Edmund H. New (John Lane); (3) rearranged and classified under subjects by Charles Mosley (Elliot Stock).

{276b} Of *Boswell's Life of Johnson* there are innumerable editions. The special enthusiast will not be happy until he possesses Dr. Birkbeck Hill's edition in 6 volumes (Clarendon Press). The most satisfactory 1 volume edition is that published on thin paper by Henry Frowde. I have in my library also a copy of the first edition of *Boswell* in 2 volumes. It was published by Henry Baldwin in 1791.

{276c} The best edition of Lockhart's *Life of Scott* is that published in 10 volumes by Jack of Edinburgh. Readers should beware of abridgments, although one of these was made by Lockhart himself. The whole eighty-five chapters are worth reading, even in the 1 volume edition published by A. & C. Black.

{276d} *Pepys's Diary* can be obtained in Bohn's Library or in Newnes' Thin Paper Classics, but Pepys should only be read under Mr. H. B. Wheatley's guidance. A cheap edition of his book, in 8 volumes, has recently been published by George Bell & Sons. I have No. 2 of the large paper edition of this book, No. 1 having gone to Pepys's own college of Brazenose, where the Pepys cypher is preserved.

{277a} Until recently one knew Walpole's *Letters* only through Peter Cunningham's edition, in 9 volumes (Bentley), and this has still exclusive matter for the enthusiast, Cunningham's Introduction to wit; but the Clarendon Press has now published Walpole's *Letters*, edited by Mrs. Paget Toynbee, in 16 volumes, or in 8. Here are to be found more letters than in any previous edition.

{277b} *The Memoirs of Count de Gramont*, by Anthony, Count Hamilton, can be obtained in splendid type, unannotated, in an edition published by Arthur L. Humphreys. A well-illustrated and well-edited edition is that published by Bickers of London and Scribner of New York, edited by Allan Fea.

{277c} Gray's *Letters*, with poems and life, form 4 volumes in Macmillan's Eversley Library, edited by Edmund Gosse.

{277d} You can obtain Southey's *Nelson*, originally written for Murray's Pocket Library as a publisher's commission, in one well-printed volume, with Introduction by David Hannay, published by William Heinemann. It should, however, be supplemented in the *Life* by Captain Mahan (2 volumes, Sampson Low & Co.), or by Professor Laughton's *Nelson and His Companion in Arms* (George Allen).

{277e} Moore's *Life and Letters of Byron* is published by John Murray in 6 volumes. It is best purchased second-hand in an old set. Moore's book must be supplemented by the 6 volumes of *Correspondence* edited by Rowland Prothero for Mr. Murray.

{278a} Sir George Trevelyan says in his *Early History of Charles James Fox* that Hogg's *Life of Shelley* is "perhaps the most interesting book in our language that has never been republished." The reproach has been in some slight measure removed by a cheap reprint in small type issued by the Routledges in 1906. The reader should, however, secure a copy of the first edition, 2 volumes, 1857. Professor Dowden, in his *Life of Shelley*, 1886, uses the book freely.

{278b} "What is the best book you have ever read?" Emerson is said to have asked George Eliot when she was about twenty-two years of age and residing, unknown, near Coventry. "Rousseau's *Confessions*," was the reply. "I agree with you," Emerson answered. But the book should not be read in a translation. The completest translation is one in 2 volumes published by Nicholls. There is a more abridged translation by Gibbons in 4 volumes.

{278c} *The Life of Carlyle*, by James Anthony Froude, which created so much controversy upon its publication, is worthy of a cheap edition, which does not, however, seem to be forthcoming. The book appeared in 4 volumes, *The First Forty Years* in 1882 and *Life in London* in 1884. It had been preceded by *Reminiscences* in 1881. Every one should read the *Letters and Memorials of Jane Welsh Carlyle*, 3 volumes, 1883. All the 9 volumes are published by the Longmans.

{279a} Samuel Rogers' *Table Talk* has been given us in two forms, first as *Recollections of the Table Talk of Samuel Rogers*, edited by Alexander Dyce, 1856, and second as *Reminiscences of Samuel Rogers*, 1859. The *Recollections* were reprinted in handsome form by H. A. Rogers, of New Southgate, in 1887, and the material was combined in a single volume in 1903 by G. H. Powell (R. Brimley Johnson). I have the four books, and delight in the many good stories they contain.

{279b} *The Confessions of St. Augustine* may be commended in many small and handy editions. One, with an Introduction by Alice Meynell, was published in 1900. The most beautifully printed modern edition is that issued by Arthur Humphreys in his Classical Series.

{279c} Amiel's *Journal* is a fine piece of introspection. A translation by Mrs. Humphry Ward is published in 2 volumes by the Macmillans. De Senancour's *Obermann*, translated by A. E. Waite (Wellby), should be read in this connexion.

{279d} *The Meditations of Marcus Aurelius*, translated by George Long, appears as a volume of Bohn's Library, and more beautifully printed in the Library of Arthur Humphreys. There are many other good translations—one by John Jackson, issued in 1906 by the Clarendon Press, has great merit.

{279e} George Henry Lewes's *Life of Goethe* has gone through many editions and remains a fascinating book, although it may be supplemented by the translation of Duntzer's *Life of Goethe*, 2 volumes, Macmillan, and Bielschowsky's *Life of Goethe*, Vols. I and II (Putnams).

{280a} *The Life of Lessing*, by James Sime, is not a great biography, but it is an interesting and most profitable study of a noble man. Lessing will be an inspiration greater almost than any other of the moderns for those who are brought in contact with his fine personality. The book is in 2 volumes, published by the Trubners.

{280b} You can read Benjamin Franklin's *Autobiography* in 1 volume (Dent), or in his Collected Works—*Memoirs of the Life and Writings of Benjamin Franklin*, edited by his grandson, William Temple Franklin, 6 volumes (Colburn), 1819. There have been at least two expensive reprints of his *Works* of late years.

{280c} *The Greville Memoirs* were published in large octavo form in the first place. Much scandal was omitted from the second edition. They are now obtainable in 8 volumes of Longmans' Silver Library. They form an interesting glimpse into the Court life of the later Guelphs.

{280d} It has been complained of John Forster's *Life of Charles Dickens* that there is too much Forster and not enough Dickens. Yet it is the only guide to the life-story of the greatest of the Victorian novelists. Is most pleasant to read in the 2 volumes of the Gadshill Edition, published by Chapman & Hall.

{280e} *The Early Diary of Frances Burney*, afterwards Madame D'Arblay, edited by Annie Raine Ellis, has just been reprinted in two volumes of Bohn's Library (Bell). We owe also to Mr. Austen Dobson a fine reprint of the later and more important *Diaries*, which he has edited in 6 volumes for the Macmillans.

{281a} The *Apologia pro Vita Sua* of John Henry Newman is one of the volumes of Cardinal Newman's *Collected Works* issued by the Longmans. It is the most interesting, and is perhaps the most destined to survive, of all the books of theological controversy of the nineteenth century.

{281b} There is practically but one edition of the *Paston Letters*, that edited by James Gairdner, of the Public Record Office, and published by the firm of Archibald Constable. The luxurious Library Edition issued by Chatto & Windus in 6 volumes should be acquired if possible.

{281c} *The Autobiography of Benvenuto Cellini* is best known in the translation of Thomas Roscoe in Bohn's Library. Mr. J. Addington Symonds, however, made a new translation, issued in two fine volumes by Nimmo.

{281d} The *Religio Medici* of Sir Thomas Browne can be obtained in many forms, although the well-to-do collector will be satisfied only with the edition edited by Simon Wilkin. The book is admirably edited by W. A. Greenhill for the "Golden Treasury Series."

Choose from Thousands of 1stWorldLibrary Classics By

A. M. Barnard
Ada Leverson
Adolphus William Ward
Aesop
Agatha Christie
Alexander Aaronsohn
Alexander Kielland
Alexandre Dumas
Alfred Gatty
Alfred Ollivant
Alice Duer Miller
Alice Turner Curtis
Alice Dunbar
Allen Chapman
Alleyne Ireland
Ambrose Bierce
Amelia E. Barr
Amory H. Bradford
Andrew Lang
Andrew McFarland Davis
Andy Adams
Angela Brazil
Anna Alice Chapin
Anna Sewell
Annie Besant
Annie Hamilton Donnell
Annie Payson Call
Annie Roe Carr
Annonaymous
Anton Chekhov
Archibald Lee Fletcher
Arnold Bennett
Arthur C. Benson
Arthur Conan Doyle
Arthur M. Winfield
Arthur Ransome
Arthur Schnitzler
Arthur Train
Atticus
B.H. Baden-Powell
B. M. Bower
B. C. Chatterjee
Baroness Emmuska Orczy
Baroness Orczy
Basil King
Bayard Taylor
Ben Macomber
Bertha Muzzy Bower
Bjornstjerne Bjornson

Booth Tarkington
Boyd Cable
Bram Stoker
C. Collodi
C. E. Orr
C. M. Ingleby
Carolyn Wells
Catherine Parr Traill
Charles A. Eastman
Charles Amory Beach
Charles Dickens
Charles Dudley Warner
Charles Farrar Browne
Charles Ives
Charles Kingsley
Charles Klein
Charles Hanson Towne
Charles Lathrop Pack
Charles Romyn Dake
Charles Whibley
Charles Willing Beale
Charlotte M. Braeme
Charlotte M. Yonge
Charlotte Perkins Stetson
Clair W. Hayes
Clarence Day Jr.
Clarence E. Mulford
Clemence Housman
Confucius
Coningsby Dawson
Cornelis DeWitt Wilcox
Cyril Burleigh
D. H. Lawrence
Daniel Defoe
David Garnett
Dinah Craik
Don Carlos Janes
Donald Keyhoe
Dorothy Kilner
Dougan Clark
Douglas Fairbanks
E. Nesbit
E. P. Roe
E. Phillips Oppenheim
E. S. Brooks
Earl Barnes
Edgar Rice Burroughs
Edith Van Dyne
Edith Wharton

Edward Everett Hale
Edward J. O'Biren
Edward S. Ellis
Edwin L. Arnold
Eleanor Atkins
Eleanor Hallowell Abbott
Eliot Gregory
Elizabeth Gaskell
Elizabeth McCracken
Elizabeth Von Arnim
Ellem Key
Emerson Hough
Emilie F. Carlen
Emily Bronte
Emily Dickinson
Enid Bagnold
Enilor Macartney Lane
Erasmus W. Jones
Ernie Howard Pie
Ethel May Dell
Ethel Turner
Ethel Watts Mumford
Eugene Sue
Eugenie Foa
Eugene Wood
Eustace Hale Ball
Evelyn Everett-green
Everard Cotes
F. H. Cheley
F. J. Cross
F. Marion Crawford
Fannie E. Newberry
Federick Austin Ogg
Ferdinand Ossendowski
Fergus Hume
Florence A. Kilpatrick
Fremont B. Deering
Francis Bacon
Francis Darwin
Frances Hodgson Burnett
Frances Parkinson Keyes
Frank Gee Patchin
Frank Harris
Frank Jewett Mather
Frank L. Packard
Frank V. Webster
Frederic Stewart Isham
Frederick Trevor Hill
Frederick Winslow Taylor

Friedrich Kerst
Friedrich Nietzsche
Fyodor Dostoyevsky
G.A. Henty
G.K. Chesterton
Gabrielle E. Jackson
Garrett P. Serviss
Gaston Leroux
George A. Warren
George Ade
Geroge Bernard Shaw
George Cary Eggleston
George Durston
George Ebers
George Eliot
George Gissing
George MacDonald
George Meredith
George Orwell
George Sylvester Viereck
George Tucker
George W. Cable
George Wharton James
Gertrude Atherton
Gordon Casserly
Grace E. King
Grace Gallatin
Grace Greenwood
Grant Allen
Guillermo A. Sherwell
Gulielma Zollinger
Gustav Flaubert
H. A. Cody
H. B. Irving
H.C. Bailey
H. G. Wells
H. H. Munro
H. Irving Hancock
H. R. Naylor
H. Rider Haggard
H. W. C. Davis
Haldeman Julius
Hall Caine
Hamilton Wright Mabie
Hans Christian Andersen
Harold Avery
Harold McGrath
Harriet Beecher Stowe
Harry Castlemon
Harry Coghill
Harry Houidini

Hayden Carruth
Helent Hunt Jackson
Helen Nicolay
Hendrik Conscience
Hendy David Thoreau
Henri Barbusse
Henrik Ibsen
Henry Adams
Henry Ford
Henry Frost
Henry James
Henry Jones Ford
Henry Seton Merriman
Henry W Longfellow
Herbert A. Giles
Herbert Carter
Herbert N. Casson
Herman Hesse
Hildegard G. Frey
Homer
Honore De Balzac
Horace B. Day
Horace Walpole
Horatio Alger Jr.
Howard Pyle
Howard R. Garis
Hugh Lofting
Hugh Walpole
Humphry Ward
Ian Maclaren
Inez Haynes Gillmore
Irving Bacheller
Isabel Cecilia Williams
Isabel Hornibrook
Israel Abrahams
Ivan Turgenev
J.G.Austin
J. Henri Fabre
J. M. Barrie
J. M. Walsh
J. Macdonald Oxley
J. R. Miller
J. S. Fletcher
J. S. Knowles
J. Storer Clouston
J. W. Duffield
Jack London
Jacob Abbott
James Allen
James Andrews
James Baldwin

James Branch Cabell
James DeMille
James Joyce
James Lane Allen
James Lane Allen
James Oliver Curwood
James Oppenheim
James Otis
James R. Driscoll
Jane Abbott
Jane Austen
Jane L. Stewart
Janet Aldridge
Jens Peter Jacobsen
Jerome K. Jerome
Jessie Graham Flower
John Buchan
John Burroughs
John Cournos
John F. Kennedy
John Gay
John Glasworthy
John Habberton
John Joy Bell
John Kendrick Bangs
John Milton
John Philip Sousa
John Taintor Foote
Jonas Lauritz Idemil Lie
Jonathan Swift
Joseph A. Altsheler
Joseph Carey
Joseph Conrad
Joseph E. Badger Jr
Joseph Hergesheimer
Joseph Jacobs
Jules Vernes
Julian Hawthrone
Julie A Lippmann
Justin Huntly McCarthy
Kakuzo Okakura
Karle Wilson Baker
Kate Chopin
Kenneth Grahame
Kenneth McGaffey
Kate Langley Bosher
Kate Langley Bosher
Katherine Cecil Thurston
Katherine Stokes
L. A. Abbot
L. T. Meade

L. Frank Baum
Latta Griswold
Laura Dent Crane
Laura Lee Hope
Laurence Housman
Lawrence Beasley
Leo Tolstoy
Leonid Andreyev
Lewis Carroll
Lewis Sperry Chafer
Lilian Bell
Lloyd Osbourne
Louis Hughes
Louis Joseph Vance
Louis Tracy
Louisa May Alcott
Lucy Fitch Perkins
Lucy Maud Montgomery
Luther Benson
Lydia Miller Middleton
Lyndon Orr
M. Corvus
M. H. Adams
Margaret E. Sangster
Margret Howth
Margaret Vandercook
Margaret W. Hungerford
Margret Penrose
Maria Edgeworth
Maria Thompson Daviess
Mariano Azuela
Marion Polk Angellotti
Mark Overton
Mark Twain
Mary Austin
Mary Catherine Crowley
Mary Cole
Mary Hastings Bradley
Mary Roberts Rinehart
Mary Rowlandson
M. Wollstonecraft Shelley
Maud Lindsay
Max Beerbohm
Myra Kelly
Nathaniel Hawthrone
Nicolo Machiavelli
O. F. Walton
Oscar Wilde

Owen Johnson
P.G. Wodehouse
Paul and Mabel Thorne
Paul G. Tomlinson
Paul Severing
Percy Brebner
Percy Keese Fitzhugh
Peter B. Kyne
Plato
Quincy Allen
R. Derby Holmes
R. L. Stevenson
R. S. Ball
Rabindranath Tagore
Rahul Alvares
Ralph Bonehill
Ralph Henry Barbour
Ralph Victor
Ralph Waldo Emmerson
Rene Descartes
Ray Cummings
Rex Beach
Rex E. Beach
Richard Harding Davis
Richard Jefferies
Richard Le Gallienne
Robert Barr
Robert Frost
Robert Gordon Anderson
Robert L. Drake
Robert Lansing
Robert Lynd
Robert Michael Ballantyne
Robert W. Chambers
Rosa Nouchette Carey
Rudyard Kipling
Saint Augustine
Samuel B. Allison
Samuel Hopkins Adams
Sarah Bernhardt
Sarah C. Hallowell
Selma Lagerlof
Sherwood Anderson
Sigmund Freud
Standish O'Grady
Stanley Weyman
Stella Benson
Stella M. Francis

Stephen Crane
Stewart Edward White
Stijn Streuvels
Swami Abhedananda
Swami Parmananda
T. S. Ackland
T. S. Arthur
The Princess Der Ling
Thomas A. Janvier
Thomas A Kempis
Thomas Anderton
Thomas Bailey Aldrich
Thomas Bulfinch
Thomas De Quincey
Thomas Dixon
Thomas H. Huxley
Thomas Hardy
Thomas More
Thornton W. Burgess
U. S. Grant
Upton Sinclair
Valentine Williams
Various Authors
Vaughan Kester
Victor Appleton
Victor G. Durham
Victoria Cross
Virginia Woolf
Wadsworth Camp
Walter Camp
Walter Scott
Washington Irving
Wilbur Lawton
Wilkie Collins
Willa Cather
Willard F. Baker
William Dean Howells
William le Queux
W. Makepeace Thackeray
William W. Walter
William Shakespeare
Winston Churchill
Yei Theodora Ozaki
Yogi Ramacharaka
Young E. Allison
Zane Grey